# BEE FOCUSED

## WHAT HONEYBEES CAN TEACH US ABOUT CHANGE, CRISIS, AND COMMUNICATION

### Scott Proposki

Published by Scott Proposki, LLC
10 Lavantie Street
Haverhill, MA 01830
www.ScottProposki.com
www.3OclockCoffee.com

Identifiers:
LLCN:
ISBN: 9781637906248 (paperback)

ISBN: 9781637906231 (Ingram Spark hardback)

Available in hardback, paperback, audiobook, and e-book.

Any internet addresses (websites, blogs, etc.) and telephone numbers printed in this book are offered as a resource. They are not intended in any way to be or imply an endorsement by the author, nor does the author vouch for the content of these sites and numbers for the life of this book.

Some names and identifying details may have been changed to protect the privacy of individuals involved.

Book layout designed by Dara Rogers - www.DarasDesign.com

# Dedication

Sometimes it's the small things that change your life forever, though you may not realize it for months or even years. Bill Thyng was a family friend who became more than a friend. To me, he was Uncle Bill. He was family.

Bill loved to go hunting, fishing, and camping in Northern Maine. For years he'd invite me to join him at his camp in the town of Jackman, but I was always too busy working—until one day I said yes. I brought my camera, of course. It helps me focus on one thing, and I was hoping to capture the northern lights.

I didn't see the northern lights, but we hiked in the woods together during that trip, and I captured a great photo of Uncle Bill in his full camouflage and hunting gear, with the epic Maine fall foliage in the background. During our trek, he was surrounded by love—his best friend, Dave Brown; his son, Mark; and, of course, me—his bonus nephew.

Looking back at that photo, you can see how focused and present Uncle Bill was that day as he spent his time with his family and friends.

Bill passed away unexpectedly mere weeks before Christmas; he was hanging wreaths around the town center for people to enjoy during the holiday session. That's the type of guy he was.

The photo I shot of him on our hike, surrounded by full-color plaques, memorial cards, and custom-framed pictures, was the focal point at his memorial.

Uncle Bill, thank you for your life lesson to "Bee Focused." My wish is that everyone will enjoy the outdoors, make time for free days away from the office, and learn new hobbies like beekeeping and fly fishing. Those pursuits will make you a well-rounded and better person, just as they did for Uncle Bill.

**In Memory of**
**William "Bill" Thyng**
**January 9, 1948–November 25, 2019**

# CONTENTS

# Praise For *Bee Focused*

"**I**t's amazing what we can learn from a honeybee to help our business focus better; I will always look at a honeybee differently now, the learning lessons in Bee Focused will help any anyone looking to focus more on your business."

– Dr. Benjamin Hardy
*Author featured in The New York Times, Forbes, Fortune, CNBC,* and the #1 most-read writer on Medium.com.

"**A**n essential read for businesses committing to thriving and navigating challenging times. What do we have to learn from successful bee hives? It turns out a lot!"

- Patti Mara
Founder of Business Reinvention Blueprint™

"**A**n essential read for businesses committing to thriving and navigating challenging times. What do we have to learn from successful bee hives? It turns out a lot!"

– Amazon Customer

"I never imaged how much I would learn about the Honeybee; Scott's simple metaphors with Honeybee and Business will help any business owner to look into the future and learn about Honeybees along the way."

– Michael Levin,
*New York Times Best Seller Author*

# Introduction
## Bee Focused
## Enjoying the Present, Planning the Future

For many years, every day at three o'clock, I'd stop whatever I was doing, get up from my desk, and meet my best friend Bobby Leblanc for coffee. Bobby and I had known each other since childhood. We were both entrepreneurs who hoped to grow our respective businesses, and we even shared an office. So why didn't we just turn to each other and chat at our desks? Because we knew if we stopped to talk whenever we felt like it, we'd get so engrossed in conversation that the rest of the day could slip away. It had happened many times before.

Instead, we started storing up all our ideas, questions, and musings for three o'clock. Then we'd get up from our desks and head out to the local café for an informal meeting. It became a tradition: our three o'clock coffee.

Bobby was an inspiring guy. He had a keen intellect and a sharp wit, and he was endlessly upbeat. He had such optimism for the future. Getting together with him outside of the office always provided the shot of adrenaline or dopamine I needed to dive into my afternoon tasks. Our three o'clock coffee date was a deeply gratifying and important ritual that helped us both reinvigorate and refocus.

In 2011, we lost Bob to pancreatic cancer. It was a devastating loss to everyone who knew him and a powerful reminder of how fragile and fleeting life can be. After Bobby passed, my need for a three o'clock coffee date was more intense than ever. Taking the time to step away from work and connect with people became increasingly important. At first, I just stopped what I was doing every day at 3 o'clock to have a coffee by myself. Then I started reaching out on social media and to other local business owners and CEOs. Eventually, I began hopping on planes to meet people all over the country for those three o'clock coffee dates.

One day I called Ron Tonini, the CEO of Picture Marketing. He developed the first Photo Booth in the '80s; he was a CEO who was focused forward, seeing the future ahead of his time. I came across his business online, and I was intrigued by what he was doing and how similar our visions were. I picked up the phone and asked if he'd be willing to meet for a 3 o'clock coffee, and to my delight, he said yes. Twenty-four hours later, I was sitting with Ron at a Caribou Coffee shop in Novato, California, 3,000 miles from my home in Massachusetts.

Ron and I hit it off right away, partly because it was instantly clear I had no ulterior motives. I wasn't trying to sell him anything or glean any insider knowledge. I only wanted to hear his personal story. Most CEOs find it hard to find someone to talk to who doesn't have a secret agenda, and I think it was refreshing for him to partake in the ritual I'd established with Bobby. We took some time simply to be together and to focus on our thoughts—our concerns with the present and our hopes for the future.

Ron was running a multimillion-dollar business, and after we sat down, the first thing he said to me was, "Scott, I'm as busy as a bee. I'm looking for some more worker bees to get it all done."

It was a great metaphor, and it was immediately apparent that finding a way to collaborate would be mutually beneficial.

What I didn't realize right away was that the honeybee metaphor was personal and meaningful to him. That night, while having dinner with Ron and his wife, Susan, I found out they were involved in their own beekeeping operation!

We talked for hours about honeybees and all the natural products derived from their hives. I could tell from their descriptions of the lavender fields that nourished the beehives and their pride in their "real" honey delicacy that beekeeping was something they were passionate about. It wasn't until the end of the night that I realized we'd never gotten around to talking about photography or business.

Nevertheless, Ron and I embarked on a joint venture that year, launching a vast photography project for Hewlett-Packard. That made us both as busy as honeybees, and I was fully immersed in my business, which was growing daily by leaps and bounds.

You can imagine my surprise when, on Christmas morning, as I was taking a much-needed break from work, I found an unexpected gift under my tree. A big white wooden box marked "fragile" was waiting for me, and my wife had a mischievous look on her face.

"What's this?" I asked her.

"Don't look at me," she said. "It was all Ron."

I ripped open the present and was shocked to find that Ron had sent me a beekeeping kit. My life as a beekeeper had officially begun.

In my book, *The Big Picture*, I write about what it means to run a business as a person who has ADHD and how a camera is a wonderful metaphor for learning how to focus. In this book, I'm excited to share another valuable frame through which you can view your business and work life: beekeeping.

In the interests of full disclosure, I'm not a professional beekeeper. I am an author, an entrepreneur, and a business advisor. Still, through all of that, I've expanded my horizons into the gratifying endeavor of hobby beekeeping. By doing so, I've learned a lot about running a business and living an enriched life.

Once I began to delve into the world of beekeeping, I began to see it everywhere. Michelle Obama had installed beehives at the White House, where I'd worked as a photographer. Many Hollywood celebrities keep their own hives. Perhaps most notable was, "Sting." Born Gordon Sumner, Sting famously got his nickname based on a yellow-and-black-striped sweater he used to wear. He's taken that one step further because, in an interview, he reveals that he is a beekeeper and that one once got the best of him.

Sting appeared on the BBC's The Graham Norton Show and was asked if he'd ever been stung. "I actually keep honeybees," he said. "I usually go and visit them just to make sure they're doing okay, cause honeybees are very stressed at the moment. They're dying out. So I go and see them, and we get along normally, but I was walking away from the hives, and a honeybee came above and stung me right on the crown of my head. And it was the most exquisite pain. It was like a psychedelic experience. ... And I haven't been the same since. It was ten years ago. Wow! Sting me again, baby."

Beekeeping must be a thing with bass players who have

insect-themed nicknames because he shares a hobby with Flea from the Red Hot Chili Peppers. Last year, the world learned that the Red Hot Chili Peppers star has approximately 200,000 bees spread out over three hives in his backyard.

It takes patience and commitment to learn about honeybees and build an environment for them. You have to respect them and be with them at the moment. You have to envision yourself as their coach, but you also must understand there will always be things beyond your control.

Every honeybee has a role, and they all work in perfect harmony to ensure the success of their shared endeavor. Honeycombs are a testament to efficiency and symmetry. The honeybees' product is always delicious and unique to the environs in which it was created.

Since I began writing this book, another powerful connection between the world of beekeeping and business has emerged: the crisis of viruses. The COVID-19 pandemic in 2020 and 2021 gripped the entire planet, and people's lives, the world economy, and our whole future were uncertain. Some businesses collapsed, while others thrived.

A similar phenomenon happens in honeybee hives. For several years we have seen outbreaks of Chronic Bee Paralysis Virus (CBPV). If the virus is not treated, the honeybees will die off, and the colony will collapse. During the COVID-19 epidemic in the United States, most businesses have had to close for months to stop the spread of this virus, and my company

---

[1]Chronic bee paralysis virus (CBPV or CPV)is an infectious and contagious disease of adult honeybees. The infection has no seasonal pattern, often remains latent, and is present in many countries. The CBPV is more frequently found in colonies infested with varroa.

was no exception. Like honeybees infected with CBPV, some companies did collapse. Still, some business owners will weather this new storm because we have to. Our ecological survival depends on the honeybees overcoming their virus. Our economic survival depends on business owners overcoming this virus.

Luckily, my experience, is that entrepreneurs, especially those with ADHD, can thrive in adverse conditions. They become focused, engaging in what people call hyper-focus, and adapt. They can pivot fast, coming up with new business ideas that respond to an altered reality. When honeybee hives get destroyed, the survivors will "bee focused" and start rebuilding the colony as soon as possible, starting from nothing, as they did once before. They never give up, and neither will we.

I have always had the unique ability to hyper-focus during adverse times; this is what makes my ADHD my "superpower." I have also learned so much from the honeybees about how to "bee focused." That new knowledge has enhanced my abilities, making me even more resilient when faced with uncertainty. Everyone has a unique superpower, and those special powers will shine during difficult times.

The more I thought about my work as a beekeeper and how my experiences have enhanced my ability to focus, the more inspired I was to apply those lessons to my life and businesses. I'm thrilled to share those observations with you at a time when they will be more useful than ever. My honeybees have sweetened my life in many ways. Like them, I've increased my efficiency. I've figured out how best to do my job and let others do theirs. I've learned how to be a hands-on coach, guiding people toward creating their best product. I've learned how to tap into my hyper-focus to enhance my resiliency. Most of all,

I've been continually reminded by my honeybees to stop and smell the roses.

As part of my book series on focus—including *Camera Focus*, *The Big Picture*, and *Focus On The Profits*—*Bee Focused* will help you prepare for a bigger and better future. It will help you envision a picture so clear and focused it becomes real. Just like the photos I once took for *National Geographic*, the White House, and HBO, the ideas in this book will help you focus on your goals to grow your business forward.

That's what Bobby and I were always trying to do with our 3 O'clock coffee time to: nurture our minds and souls so we could be better at achieving our visions for the future. Those coffee dates led me to beekeeping in a roundabout way and to some of the most important discoveries about focus I've ever made. I'm thrilled to share some of those discoveries with you in this book.

I think Bob would be proud. Today I have turned 3 O'clock Coffee into a podcast that can be found on Spotify, Amazon Music, Apple, Audible, and many other podcast platforms. In my podcast, I focus on extraordinary people sharing meaningful stories and ideas in business and in life that will inspire you. www.3OclockCoffeePodcast.com

# To Bee or Not to Bee

There's nothing like the first time ten thousand honeybees surround you. Not that a second time is any more charming, but it's the sheer terror that grips one's heart when such an encounter takes place for the first time. Words do not do justice to the experience as you can never convey to someone how nerve-racking it is to stand next to ten thousand honeybees looking to sting you. Yet, despite the sheer terror you experience, your heart threatening to jump out of your chest, you feel compelled to take a closer look; perhaps get a closer look at the hive, or if you are a kid, maybe even catch one to show it to your parents back home. It is supposedly their indulgence in their work that makes us think they may not harm us, but a slip of judgment and you may find yourself scratching multiple parts of your body furiously as the sting kicks in.

Honeybees are a unique type of insect such that their work is fundamentally necessary for our ecosystem to thrive. If you don't do right by them, they make sure you pay dearly for your actions.

Imagine that you're fully suited up—gloves on, tight white

elastics bound around your wrists, zipper pulled tightly all the way above your chin, top veil mask over your head, and a hazard suit wrapped around your body that makes you look like you're about to blow up the whole world using a radioactive explosive. Oh, and did I mention the fear and adrenaline pumping through your veins? Depending on your motive for surrounding yourself with countless honeybees, the moment can be either be exhilarating or absolutely terrifying. There is no in-between. Like any animal, honeybees mind their own business until provoked. So the visual of the honeybees merely swarming around randomly changes immediately the moment you begin to offend them. Instead of random, erratic motion, their movement becomes organized, almost as if with purpose. If one could ever pause that moment to observe this change, you would witness the marvelous, instinctive force which drives them to do their work. Of course, in reality, this plan would never work out, as you would find yourself with red splotches all over your body before you could even glance up at them. Regardless, the magnificent formation and discipline in which the swarm organizes itself are genuinely remarkable.

Now come to the real part: handling a swarm with your bare hands. Beekeeping is perhaps one of the most patience-necessary jobs. The level of calm you have to maintain as you look at the collection of daunting, flying insects is perhaps the most important part of this job. Your brain starts humming, but you're completely focused on the task at hand. You take out the brand new bee box you bought. The only thing separating you and the honeybees is a small net. You pull out your bee smoker, a device used in beekeeping to calm honeybees. It is designed to generate smoke from the smoldering of various fuels, hence the name. It is designed as a stainless steel cylinder with a lid that narrows to a gap with a half-inch diameter. They're about to go for a ride, and you don't want to give them too good of a time.

As you slowly open the lid, the honeybees seem paralyzed, but a few break out. Your brain is humming and trying to focus on the honeybees who fly by in random trajectories, not allowing your eyes to focus on them. Focus on the job; do not let yourself get intimidated. Then you snap out of it and realize you have to be focused entirely on the task at hand. These honeybees are not your concern at the moment. I suppose this step can be compared to an example that is common in most of our lives. You strive for a goal; this may be a good job, a dream university, or anything else. The path you take to achieve that goal is long, tedious, and filled with obstacles, but you deal with them as you go. However, one of the more insignificant parts of your journey, which unfortunately ends up having a big impact, will be the opinions of people. They may try to bring you down, talk behind your back, or demean your efforts, but would you consider them essential things to focus on, given the task at hand? Would you focus on achieving your goal or listening to their views on your life? I suppose the answer would be typical for most of us. Hence, this is how the swarm of honeybees should be approached—in view of your goal, which is finding the queen bee.

However, before this, you need to take a few precautionary measures; wait for dawn to relocate the hive so all the honeybees have returned. Now, you need to set aside your queen, which you must carefully do. Many times, it might not be that easy finding the big royalty under the buzzing storm of all the others. You might have to search for a while, maybe looking around in the nearest areas to find her. However, she can be characterized exclusively. Aside from the fact that she is the largest honeybee of the hive, she will be seen to have wings that only make it halfway down to her abdomen instead of all the other bees that have wings fully covering their abdomens. If you have a keen eye, you might even notice the most important pattern: all the other bees will appear to be facing their queen, following her, sheltering her, and swarming all around her in protectiveness. However, once you find Miss Royalty, the procedure is pretty simple from here.

All royalty deserves their own protocol, and so you put the queen in a separate chamber. This chamber is large enough to let the worker bees fly out but not enough to let the queen out. Most beekeepers use a screen called the queen excluder to keep the queen in the hive's lower boxes. This prevents the honeybee from laying eggs in the upper chambers, where the beekeepers shake the frames to collect the honey. You need to make sure not to make aggressive gestures but rather gently ease the queen honeybee into her chamber of solitude. She's unique and needs to be treated like a VIP. Plus, if you make her upset, you'll be paying for it dearly. You make sure that no unwanted guests accompany her by brushing her off. For this, slightly shake the queen bee separator to fly off any other honeybees accompanying her. She is then safely escorted to her solitude. You'll have time for her later. Now comes the daring part. Even with protection, playing with honeybees is like diving headfirst into infested waters. One wrong move, and you have no idea what will come at you.

For now, you slowly remove the innermost frames from the hive to create some space for the new honeybees that you're about to put in. You dive in, slowly making sure the hive is clear before you execute your plan.

Your goal is to transfer the honeybees from your box to their new hive, and you make sure to take as many steps as you can to do that safely.

You start shaking the honeybee box aggressively so the honeybees are woken up. Of course, they don't take too kindly to your actions and start buzzing around you. Keep reminding yourself that you have protective clothing on, and the bees won't sting you so you don't get sidetracked from your goal. Now, for the first time, you're surrounded by thousands of honeybees circling your body and dancing around you. You feel their energy from the haphazard yet lightning-fast movements and the buzzing sound they make. The buzzing of thousands of honeybees gets overwhelming, and your heart beats faster, sinking you more in fear by the minute. You could put a sign in neon light, and they would still ignore it to confront you. You've awakened them from their slumber, and they want to give you a piece of their mind. You feel their energy. You hear their buzzing. You sense them all around you, full of life. It's beautiful in a way to be observing a process so full of life and organized; a small change of nature, and there is a rapid response.

You probably have a question in your mind right now, and so

it is best to answer it beforehand. No, they can't sting through the fancy suit you're wearing. However, if you startle them enough, they will go out of their way to find an opening to capitalize, and trust me when I tell you that is not in your best interest. No matter how honeybee-proof your suit is, they will try to find an Achilles heel and make you pay, and so monitor your movements. Do not try to dump the honeybees hastily from one place to the other. You must treat them gently as if caressing a young child in its early years.

Once the honeybees swarm around you, at that moment, you aren't thinking about anything but avoiding stings. In a way, they have your life in their hands, and you have to pay them the respect and attention they deserve; to treat the hive in a manner worthy of the royalty of her Highness, the queen bee. This moment will stand in your memory forever—the same way you remember the day you got married, the day you opened the doors to your business, or the day your first child was born. It's truly a creative experience.

As the honeybees are hovering around you at full force, looking for an opening, this is the moment where the doubt starts to creep in. Did I wear the suit completely? Are the gloves still tight? Is my face still covered? What if they find a patch behind me? The moment your mind shifts in pondering in that direction, you need to shake it back. You must start to focus on the task at hand. The honeybee box still has half the honeybees stuck in it. You have doused them with too much smoke, and they're still groggy. You must act before the bees charge up and decide they did not appreciate the smoke in such a manner.

Now you must transfer the honeybees to their new home. Often, nature will do the job for you. You just need to let gravity do the job to make the honeybees fall into the new hive you have set up for them. If gravity isn't doing the job, you need to give them a slight push.

Tilting the box as much as you can, you lean in to see if the honeybees fall from the container into their hive. It's not working. You start to vibrate the box back and forth slowly. The lumps stuck in the sides begin to carve off. It's still not enough, though. You need to go the extra step. You simply shake the box once, and the honeybees are dumped into the hive. Of course, they don't take too kindly to that and start coming at you with everything they've got. You have shaken their box a few times, and they are starting to realize that some external force is interfering with their work. Think of the bees like workaholics; you try to shake them up from their routine job and are met with aggression.

However, you can't afford to panic once again because the job is far from finished. There's still plenty of honeybees left that need to be transferred into the hive. Looking the other way, you muster up the courage to give the box another tap, and all remainder of the honeybees finally land into the new hive. You scrape a few honeybees off the corners with your trusty brush. With most of the honeybees gone, the task is finally done. Now, to close the deal, you bring back the queen from her exile and carefully place her inside the hive in a particular container. She is separated from the other honeybees in a container with a small hole blocked with sugar that the worker bees will remove in a few days as soon as you introduce her Highness. Now you finally take a long breath and sigh in relief; the hard part is over. With everything in place, you place the lid on top of the honeybee hive and seal the deal.

*So, why honeybees?*

In the years since Ron shared his great gift of beekeeping with me, I've often wondered, *How did he know to send me honeybees?* It's not as if a beehive kit was on the top of my bucket list. As I opened the package, however, much to my shock, I found an array of unfamiliar-looking structures which could easily pass off as spare boxes left in the garage over the span of years. As I looked through them, I flipped through a guide to identifying which structure was what. There was a honeybee veil and a hive tool, the function of both I was still totally unaware of. A honeybee smoker and honeybee smoker fuel accompanied the package, which frankly seemed bizarre to me. Why would you want to smoke many insects that would take any chance to spec your body with unbearable rashes? I did not know. There was one familiar item in the box, and that was a pair of gloves for the beekeeping suit. Coming to the most important part of the kit, there were ten wax foundation sheets, one frame of wooden super, an inner cover, and an entrance feeder. There were also ten top bar frames and a bottom board. The most haunting part about this kit was that it was entirely unassembled. This would take years!

And then came the fun part—the honeybees. The package consisted of a box with screens in the side and the queen honeybee in a cage at the top of the package and honeybees on the upper, inner surface of the box. Inside the package, was feed to keep the honeybees alive. I was excited and yet did not know what to make of it. A thousand honeybees in a box was quite overwhelming. Ron had, of course, told me about beekeeping, but I didn't expect him to send a hive and a box with 10,000 honeybee workers to my doorstep. The reason never occurred to me, but it did not stop me wondering. After all, many CEOs might have presumed golf clubs or a tennis racket would be an appropriate Christmas gift. Somehow, Ron knew the honeybees would speak to me as they had to him. It begs the question of what gave it away? How did it occur to Ron that, as with him, honeybees could connect and speak with me as well?

For the most part, the truth is that a game of golf or tennis is usually a networking opportunity for business people. It serves as a quick time-out session for the self-erected businesses. It allows such busy-as-honeybee-professionals to take a step out from their busy schedule and meet and greet each other. It can very well be an exercise and technically a "hobby." Still, it's often really just an excuse to get together with colleagues and clients outside of the office—just like a honeybee buzzing away from the flowers with other worker bees. However, golf or tennis can never really compare to the thrill of the art of beekeeping. It's thrilling in the sense of how the honeybees present danger, and the intricate layers of detailing involved to be a good beekeeper make it a much more attractive "sport" than golf or tennis.

Beekeeping is an activity that is truly separate from everything else. As far as I can recollect, there is no parallel to beekeeping. You have to give it your undivided attention or risk getting stung. In a way, not only do the honeybees demand your attention, but they also seek you out and make you attend to them using their twisted way of attacking you. I like to call it my way of living on the edge! For the first few months, it's not a social activity at all. You can't simply invite people over to have a look because for the first few months after you decide to get a hive, the new honeybees need time to adapt and settle into their environment. Honeybees are intelligent creatures and use their cognitive abilities to measure speed and distance, and they also use polarized light to determine their compass direction. This helps the new honeybees detect that their home has changed. It is advised to buy honeybees from your local areas so as not to trigger a lot of aggression from the tiny insects for having changed their position.

Nevertheless, it is best for the first few months to let the honeybees adapt to their new environment and not make a show sport out of them by calling spectators. Although, after some time and experience, you may be able to invite spectators to join, that's only if you know what you're doing. My dad, for example, loves to hang around for days when I populate the hive—but it's not exactly an opportunity to update clients on your fourth-quarter numbers. The honeybees demand your full focus, and you have to be present with them for everything to work safely.

For me, and for many other people, this shift of focus from my business work to a captivating, fun, and challenging hobby is essential to the business' success.

Yes, I can hear you scoffing: "Wait, what? Is a hobby essential to the success of your *business*? Are the two even related?"

The answer for many of us is yes, they are. For a person like me, who has the ability and impulse to be hyper-focused on the task at hand, if I don't diversify my attention in one way or another, the burnout rate is high. Unlike the honeybees, I can't afford to be focused on one thing alone. I need to expand my horizons and be able to juggle multiple endeavors. Think of it this way. If I can lift a large, heavy box, it doesn't mean I can hold it for eternity. Sooner or later, I'm going to have to drop it and shift my attention to something else. Otherwise, my hands will get worn out, and the same box that I could lift will start feeling heavier and larger. The same can be said with your work-life balance. Tending to honeybees gives me an escape from my own mind, which drags me along with my useful thoughts in full circles. It can also be argued that beekeeping is a task that requires attention to detail and precision and enables us to master the art of losing ourselves in the process of doing something. This may seem like an absurd way to relax, but sometimes we need an activity that does not challenge our brain's intellectual part, but rather just the practical.

It is a much-known fact that business owners tend to obsess about their work. Over the years, their brains have become wired to think about success and ways to achieve it constantly. Wherever they are and go to, their thoughts never relinquish chasing success, and it does not matter if they are in an office environment or at home. Their mind is always revolving around their work. I mean, who can blame them? The success of the

66 **beekeeping is a task that requires attention to detail and precision and enables us to master the art of losing ourselves in the process of doing something.** 99

company often lies entirely in their hands. It lies in their ability to make the right decisions at the right time. It lies in their ability not only to keep up but to capitalize on trends and market shifts. And, yes, it lies in their willingness to work their tails off.

Still, all work and no play contribute to a tedious journey, especially when the objective remains crystal clear, but the path leading to it is obscured. That is a major problem people underestimate. In my last two books, *Camera Focus* and *The Big Picture*, I talk frankly about my ADHD. This isn't meant to be a sales pitch (although I do suggest you check it out). Still, I describe in depth how I've come to view it as a gift, how it helps drive me, and how it has become a boon to my business by employing the right techniques. It's about recognizing the tools available at your disposal and then engaging them in the best possible way to produce something remarkable.

You can check the books out, but for context, ADHD (Attention Deficit Hyperactivity Disorder) is essentially when someone has a hard time concentrating on things. It can vary from something as small as leg jiggling to losing all of your attention during a big speech. It can even mean interrupting people, and being too impatient to finish their sentences is very common.

Still, those who do have it know what I'm talking about and where I'm coming from. It also motivated me to want to be above my condition, however, and to prove to myself that I can still control the incidents of my life on my own terms.

I know it may seem easier said than done, but embracing

your capacity, no matter how high or low, and then finding workarounds is the only way to move forward. People don't often realize that because it's effortless for me to lose attention in crucial moments, it can also mean that it's hard to go back once I get fixated. When I'm in the zone, it can be difficult for me, like for many entrepreneurs, to pull away from something that has captured my attention. Don't get me wrong; it's a good feeling to be hyper-focused; it's just that the inability to thrust yourself out of it kills the advantage. You might find yourself in a situation where you feel burnt out but lack the ability to pull yourself out of it. Unfortunately, the counter to this is also an extreme; once you're out of the zone, it's hard to get back in it. That is why having this kind of tunnel vision can make you successful, but it also can drain your energy, inspiration, and zest for your business.

The thought process ADHD secretly builds in my head, without a doubt, serves me for the better. However, suppose I keep it unchecked or don't keep myself distracted. In that case, I fall into the loophole of thinking about just one task at hand while ignoring all the things around me in the process. Having engaging side projects and hobbies is essential for recharging your batteries. That is why, at least for me, beekeeping has become a perfect outlet.

One thing to keep in mind is that having such complementary inspiration isn't only for people with ADHD. Cultivating outside interests is important for *everyone*, whether you're the CEO or a student studying at university. We all have goals, and sometimes in the pursuit of these goals, you trick your mind into believing it is entirely okay for you to be working and doing nothing else. You want to think this strategy will bear fruit and the end product will be worth it. While this is an admirable quality, and while you may even succeed in achieving that goal, there may come a time where you find yourself unable to want to make this hustle again. This phase may come after years of uninterrupted work, but it restricts your ability to start new projects once it does. Therefore, it is important to make consistent efforts but also to allow yourself to vent out.

I believe in continuing to learn and educate myself as I move forward. Taking a step back and focusing on myself helps me to adjust my center and leap ahead accordingly. Just as I enjoy reaching out to help other people, I find that seeking advice and camaraderie with other business owners is the key to longevity. You can only listen to your advice for so long. Sometimes it's a good idea to hear everyone else's outlook. Over the years, interacting with CEOs of all different kinds, representing various sizes of businesses, I've made a startling discovery. Not all CEOs are very happy doing what they do. This may have to do with the long hours of the hustle and bustle daily or that many such CEOs continuously indulge in moving forward without taking a step back. Sometimes you need to have some space, reflect on yourself, and plan the future accordingly. As mentioned earlier, learning and educating oneself now and then helps in preparing the way forward.

A buzzword that's pretty common these days, is the word *coach* in connection with everything. There are fitness coaches, mindfulness coaches, life coaches, business coaches, and even gaming coaches. People seem to have caught on to the value of having consistent mentorship in many different areas. Of course, having coaches can drastically improve one's progress in whatever task one is trying to accomplish. It doesn't hurt to have a safety net underneath you, however, and a net that bounces you back into that direction can come in handy. You don't need a coach or an "expert" for everything you do in life. This is because, while a coach only gives you the principles to implement in your work, the student often ends up adopting the personality or the methods of the mentor. While this is not necessarily a bad thing, it does pose some threats to individuality and the process of one's critical thinking. Therefore, it is good to do some things on your own in life.

The concept of coaching was almost non-existent around twenty-five years ago when many of the most successful CEOs of today were starting. Being great wasn't always this accessible. The entire concept of being great was different. Some of these people have been in business for decades, and in that time, they've grown multimillion-dollar companies. Plenty of them have also gone bankrupt once or twice. Most have been divorced and remarried more than once. Many have suffered from addiction to all kinds of stuff, and some have even attempted suicide.

The life of a CEO isn't as glamorous and luxurious as you'd think. It's incredibly stressful, and a single mistake can turn years of asset building into a pile of dust. What can all this be attributed to? Many factors affect a person's life, and the world of business comes with extreme pressures. If it were so simple and easy, everyone would be starting a business and enjoying success, but of course, it's not. If I'd been given a chance to coach some of these people when they were starting out, one of my main pieces of advice would've been, "Find a hobby."

Yes, that's how much I value the idea of keeping a hobby. Granted, not many would've taken me seriously, but I'd echo the advice as many times as I could. Get a hobby, a side gig, anything fun that can help you escape the world that you're in right now.

For many CEO's, their lives consisted of business, business, and more business, with some extra business added on the weekends. I'm joking somewhat, but it's also serious. Imagine what it's like to build a big company. Imagine the effect that must have had on their health and relationships. Entrepreneurs are driven, *focused* individuals, and most of their time and energy is spent turning their dream into a reality. In their mind, the professional success they seek isn't a goal but a necessity. Had they cultivated some activity outside of their business, they might have succeeded more in other areas as well. Instead, they're so involved in business aspects that they fail to see it from any different perspective. This breeds ground for an uncreative and soul-consuming environment that ends up gobbling everything it sees.

Here's a question to consider when you're having a hard time tearing yourself away from work to engage in a recreational activity: What's worth more to you—time or money? Think about it. You can grab a piece of pen and paper to narrow down all the things you like doing in your life or something you want to do in life. Which ones need money to be accomplished? Which ones need more time to be accomplished? Which ones need a bit of both? Once you're done with your theory, allow me to present mine. You can always make more money, but you can't make more time.

It's not rocket science. We all know this to be true, yet we seldom act on it. Time is money goes the saying, but money would be worth time as well if that were entirely true. We know that's not the case. Are we able to focus on what's in front of us? I am fortunate enough to have a vacation home. When I first started going up north to my home in New Hampshire on the weekends, I'd bring my computer and many business books with me. No matter where I was, work wasn't very far away. Then I realized I don't want to be distracted by outside things when I'm at work, and I shouldn't be distracted by work when I am away from the office on the weekends. When you mingle either with each other, you fail to focus on any of them. It's pretty simple, but it took me a while to figure that out. Do everything in life to its maximum potential, be it work or leisure. If you are working, remove distractions, and focus solely to put in the best work you can. The same goes for relaxation. Stop worrying about work for a moment, and let yourself have this piece of feeling at peace.

I mentioned that the vacation home in New Hampshire is now filled with books on subjects like camping and fly-fishing. I've gotten pretty good at fly-fishing. It has further expanded the conversations I'm able to have when I meet people. There is only so much you can talk about with people when it's related to work. Knowing outside the confines of your office and its corporate building is the real deal. Maybe that will be a future book: *Fish Focus*.

## Creating a well-rounded lifestyle

It takes work to maintain a well-rounded lifestyle and to be a well-rounded person, but there are many reasons to do that work. For one, you're going to be a lot more fun at parties. In the past, I was known in every situation as "the camera guy." Having shot for *National Geographic*, the White House, Microsoft, and Google, I have great stories about my experiences as a photographer. Increasingly, because of my first book, I'm also known as "the focus guy," and people want to ask me questions about that. While I certainly have a deep and abiding interest in both of those topics, the question I'd get asked most often was some variation of, "My uncle wants to buy a camera. Any suggestions on which one he should get?"

Not only is that boring to me, but there are other problems with being associated only with your business. You are unintentionally aligned with the industry, making everything you say become a potential sales pitch. People are always wondering if you're trying to sell them something. Nobody wants to feel like they're constantly being sold to, which is why TV commercials are universally despised. If you have nothing to talk about aside from work, it makes you seem flat; nobody likes flat things—even curvy roads are more fun to drive on.

One day I was fortunate to be with some incredible masterminds—business owners and CEOs of hundred-million-dollar companies, maybe a few billionaires. They were spending time with me. I felt like I was fulfilling one of my lifelong goals: to be surrounded by people more intelligent than me. It's not that I like feeling inferior to more competent people. It's the opposite. I like surrounding myself with people with different ideas and outlooks on life to learn new things and challenge myself continually. Besides, it's always a good feeling to feel like you are being associated with a brilliant, accomplished group of people.

That day, somehow, the topic steered into the direction of my honeybees. I was so intrigued by all types of questions about honeybees. People asked me, "You're a *what*?" I would show them photos of my hives, they would ask questions, and before I knew it, other people were cutting into the conversation: "Well, where do you find the honeybees?" "How much honey do you produce?" "How did you get started?" It was an icebreaker that allowed me to meet dozens of different people and have healthy and fun conversation with them. None of them felt I was trying to sell them something, and the conversations exchanged were genuine. Plus, I would not want to admit it, but it was a much more animated conversation than having to talk about work, corporate, and business all the time.

I mean, these were people who were brilliant at what they did, the best minds in their industries, and among the most successful and wealthiest people in the world. Yet here I had knowledge they didn't possess, and that made me interesting to them. So suddenly, I had the power dynamic in the palm of my hand as I became interested in them. I found out beekeeping was something unique among that crowd, and if something is unique, it will get attention. If you have a unique business, you're going to have a thriving business.

When I began my beekeeping adventure, I knew I couldn't do it without some firm guidance and mentorship. I took a class, but I also wanted to find a beekeeping mentor. I was lucky enough to cross paths with Todd Barker from Oxford, MA, who remains my honeybee mentor to this day. If I have a problem, question, or ambition, Todd is always there to talk about it thoroughly. He helped me foresee certain obstacles so I could avoid them, and he has also fielded a few last-minute, panicked calls from me ("Um, Todd ... my honeybees just swarmed, what do I do?"). Without a mentor like Todd, I probably wouldn't have as much knowledge, my hives wouldn't be quite as thriving, and I certainly wouldn't have had as much fun doing this as I do now.

As with beekeeping, a good mentor can make or break your success in business. That's why I believe in coaching. Whatever business you're in, having people who are genuinely there to help you thrive is essential, just as Todd helped me navigate the ins and outs of the honeybee world as a hobby. Then you can put in your initiative to the basics that have been taught to you—your personalized twist to any work.

## Getting past the discomfort

When I started getting into beekeeping, I also took my foot off the gas of my business a bit. I was experiencing something many business owners feel once their business hits the ceiling: a sort of complexity fatigue. This is the feeling you get when things are going well, but you've hit your boundary for growth. If you plan to grow any more, you have to make some fundamental changes—whether that's more investment, franchising, expansion, or diversification. You can't afford to have stagnancy hinder the growth of your prospect, so something needs to be done. All of these options can be exciting, but they might also make a person *very* uncomfortable. With every action comes an equal and opposite reaction. Expansion isn't always a positive endeavor as it adds more complications like maintenance and advanced management. In my case, the idea of growing bred discomfort and inspired me to take a step back and throw myself into my newly discovered hobby of beekeeping.

Think about that. I was feeling uncomfortable, so I immersed myself in *honeybees*.

I can't tell you if it was a well-thought-out, rational choice at the moment, but it worked for me. It was almost as if I had to practice being uncomfortable in a different environment before applying it to my business. Putting on that suit and heading into a beehive was an exercise in discomfort for me. I was pushing myself both mentally and physically.

In the early days, sometimes I'd just put the suit on and stand outside the hive, too nervous about stepping in. I would stare at the hive, trying to focus, repeating to myself, "I can do this, I can do this."

A few seconds later, I'd tell myself, "I can't do this." Then I'd take off the suit and walk away; I would take a shot of Jack Daniels to calm my nerves, which ok, was maybe not the best of life decisions, but at the time, it seemed appropriate.

It wasn't the time; I wasn't ready. There was no forcing it. I had to repeat that routine quite a few times until I built up my confidence level. I had to create a level of comfort before I could proceed by going through the motions and taking small steps toward my goal. It is always a daunting task to step into something foreign. Many people choose not to do it at all. To be fair, change does not come naturally to most of us. Dangling our feet into a pit of something unknown feels uncomfortable, but it is only when we step out of our comfort zone bubble that we grow the most. You can't expect to grow and learn while sitting in the proximity of the four walls of your house or your familiar friends. It would be best to branch out, explore, and maybe even get disappointed to learn new things. Now I have five hives, and I walk around them with complete confidence. (Not complete, but a lot of confidence).

Many entrepreneurs can relate to this. When you start your business, you're consumed with a burst of passion and excitement for an idea. Once you've made it work, you'll come to that inevitable crossroads where you have to decide, "What's next?" It's an uncomfortable place to be, and sometimes you need to sit there for a while before you can move forward.

In my case, I took a step back and dove into my side hobby as a way of taking the pressure off and reassessing my situation. Going forward at full throttle doesn't always guarantee progression. Sometimes slowing down is the way to go. Not only is beekeeping full of metaphors useful for entrepreneurs, but it was a great distraction, as I learned to be comfortable with being uncomfortable in my growth.

You don't need to have a rocket strapped to your back with you aiming for the sky at all times. Sometimes it's okay to take it slow and steady with expansion. I would never have dreamed I would write a book, much less three or four books, but once I took the leap and wrote my first book, I got past those growing pains. Uncomfortable has become the new comfort for me, which will be the way for you as well once you move past the initial phase of hurt and uneasiness. Push through the initial phase of worry and uncertainty; anything new is daunting, but once you fall into the habit of wanting new experiences, you are good to go.

There are a lot of knee-jerk reactions to feeling uncomfortable. You can, of course, quit directly, which isn't recommended. It's better to test the waters thoroughly before abandoning the ship, and leaving halfway will not accomplish that. Another reaction is to endure the uncomfortable and incorporate it into your norm. This works for some, but I don't recommend it either. If you start living a life you don't feel happy in, it's not a life worth living now, is it? The third—and my preferred way—is to step back and embrace the uncomfortable. Find out what's causing the problem, and figure out a way to fix it.

Most of us feel uncomfortable having started something new because we do not have expertise in that area, which naturally makes us slightly inadequate in that field. Some sort of failure in the newly adopted field would naturally end up depressing you further. However, this is rarely the time to quit and go back to what you already know. This is the time to say, "Okay, how can I be better?" And so, you start finding mentors, reading up, or asking for help. This will improve your communication skills and help you get through your newly adopted activity. Many people, especially those who have succeeded in fostering a business empire, feel they do not need help. This may not necessarily be because of ego. Still, it can also be because setting up a business requires quite a lot of vision.

I encourage people to focus on one minute at a time when they start to feel it. Find a way to sit in your discomfort. Get used to it. Work up to the big changes moment by moment. Eventually, you start to see through the discomfort, and it becomes a way of life, not so uncomfortable after all. Instead, it becomes invigorating.

## Creating an environment

For a hive to do well, the honeybees have to have the right environment. This is affected by several factors: the position of the hive, the weather, the preponderance of pollen in the surrounding area, the interaction of honeybees with other creatures and objects —any number of things can affect the output. This output can be as worldly as extracting honey to taking care of your worker bees, your queen, and even the equipment itself. Inside, the hive is organized to function like clockwork. Every single honeybee knows its job and does it

---

[2]Source: https://www.facebook.com/214003275307497/photos/a.233362006704957/1145 256952182120/?type=3

efficiently. If you've seen a honeycomb, you know what I'm talking about. If not, I'd check it out online. It's pretty visually stimulating. It's a perfectly symmetrical product of nature, created by millions of years of workplace evolution. This fact stresses the importance of maintaining your hives and also your honeybees. In certain situations, you may need to re-queen the hive. Some indicators which point to this are when the queen bee stops producing sufficient eggs. Another one of the factors which define hive maintenance is the weather. Extreme cold or extremely hot weather may affect the combs and the honeybees alike and lead to problems in honey collecting and the actual working of the honeybees. It is essential to make sure the hive is not only surviving but also thriving. There's a reason "honeybees" are synonymous with "productivity."

As a beekeeper, you need to create an atmosphere conducive to success, which depends on many factors. It's not as simple as amassing a bunch of honeybees and asking them to work hard. That's not going to cut it. The same can be said for you and your business.

Part of establishing a positive atmosphere is creating a fantastic workspace. Have you ever gone into an office that has an odd odor? In a world of windowless cubicles, fluorescent lighting, and buzzing snack machines, it's no wonder it can be hard to motivate and inspire workers.

In my office, I've been extra careful to create an environment in which my team members can thrive. Yes, I refer to all employees as team members. It helps create a bond, and we're not a bunch of zombie employees. My office is painted a gorgeous red. It's carefully organized in an aesthetically pleasing way. It's full of artful photographs, and we even have a small café with some of the best coffee around. There's a spirit of fun and camaraderie in our space and a sense that we're all in it together. I'm convinced that has a significant effect on employee loyalty and the quality of our product.

So, did you know honey can taste wildly different depending on where it's from? If your local flower is lavender, the honey will taste different from a hive near roses, tulips, or blueberries. If the flowers are frail or in short supply, the honey will suffer. The same is true of your workforce. You'll infuse the work with whatever you choose to place in the environment. If it's gloomy and depressing, your output will be as well. If it's bright and forward-looking, you can expect the same for your business. The same principle applies to treatment. If your workers are treated well, appreciated, and constantly rewarded for their hard work, the motivation to do good work will show. Similarly, if you take care of the hive, reposition it, keep it clean and well-nourished, your worker bees will ensure high-quality honey.

## A job for every bee, a bee for every job

There's a slogan that the NFL New England Patriots football head coach Bill Belichick uses that I often come back to: "Do your job." It sounds simple, doesn't it? You can see his players adhere to that notion and in their multiple Super Bowls wins over the years (yes, love them or hate them, that's Super Bowls, plural). No one has fulfilled that slogan as expertly as former quarterback Tom Brady. I've always been in awe of his performance and his sheer focus. I was also surprised to learn Tom Brady was a beekeeper when he lived in Boston. He would occasionally post family photos to his 60,000 followers on his Instagram account. On one Memorial Day weekend, he posted a picture of him and his kids sporting iconic white honeybee suits,

**"A whole lot of love (and honeybees) in the air today at the Brady household!—with Gisele Bündchen." - Tom Brady[2]**

A beehive functions like a champion sports team in that way. Every honeybee focuses on its job, whether it's a worker bee, whose job is to forage and pollinate; a drone bee, who's there to mate with the queen; or the queen bee, whose job is to lay eggs to populate the hive. Of course, most businesses are more complicated than your average beehive, with many more kinds of jobs and more levels of stratification. Still, just like a beehive, if you're the CEO, you're counting on all your workers to do their jobs. If you hire an accountant, you don't want that person answering the phones or designing your packaging. That person is there to focus on their specific job and to be a part of the whole team. And so, this is where the task designations in a beehive come into play. Worker bees are assigned for almost all of these tasks, but they only live for about 4-6 weeks. This is when the tasks are passed down to the new set of worker bees. Some of these tasks include ventilating the hive, feeding larvae, defending the hive, and tending to the queen and the drones.

When I started my photography business, I was very busy taking pictures, as one might imagine. But as it grew, I found I had less time to take pictures and started to lose interest. I had been through the phase of being a physical photographer so much that it didn't appeal to me that much anymore. I wanted to focus on the next strategic move, how to grow, and share what I'd learned with other interested people. My job had changed from taking pictures to running the company so others could take those pictures. I first had to find the right worker bees to populate my hive. Once I did that, I was free to focus on the new tasks that had surfaced. I was free to do my job, as Bill Belichick would've encouraged me to do.

You'll encounter different kinds of workers in your role as CEO. Sometimes they'll be like worker bees, content to do their job day in and day out with no desire to change. Sometimes they'll be more ambitious, hoping to grow and move up in the company. Both kinds of people are essential to the success of your business. What you need to do is understand your employees. You need to understand their mentality, their limits, their dynamics, their strengths and weaknesses, and of course, their goals. With a proper understanding of who they are and what they want, you can help them with their goals and, in turn, help them reach yours. Many CEOs do not understand this concept. They prepare a list of things they want to be executed and assign it with no reference or area for suggestions. The best leader is one who can be flexible and alternate between different types of leadership. There is an autocratic leadership where the leader decides individually. At the same time, there is also a democratic or a people's leader who takes votes and makes decisions based on popular opinion. While both types are suitable for specific case scenarios, it is in the business's best interest to have a leader whose style to adopt in which method. For instance, it may be best to adopt an autocratic style in high-risk situations to avoid delays in making decisions. In contrast, it may be in good interest to consult other people while making decisions that directly affect many people.

Nevertheless, I've found great joy and wisdom in beekeeping. Throughout this book, I'll use it as a metaphor for achieving more extraordinary things with your business and your life. Of course, beekeeping isn't for everyone. It requires a significant investment of money, time, and space. As you read on, imagine immersing yourself in a hobby like beekeeping, one that will absorb your attention for the whole time you're participating. What would it do for your mind to be fully engaged in something outside of your business? What new skill or world would you want to learn about? What would you love to do if given a chance?

Maybe it's time to give yourself that opportunity.

On the next page are some things to keep in mind as you launch into your new adventure.

 **Buzzing Points**

• Finding a hobby that demands your focus can be great for your business. Having engaging side projects and hobbies is essential for recharging your batteries.

• If you are someone who gets hyper-focused, the burnout rate of your attention can be high. It's essential to diversify your interests.

• Many CEOs are unhappy because the only thing is their business, and their whole existence is predicated on success.

• You can always make more money. You cannot make more time.

• Nobody wants to feel like you're only talking to them to sell something. Cultivating outside interests will allow you to engage with people in authentic ways.

• Find a mentor or coach you can trust.

• When you've hit a ceiling of growth, you may experience complexity fatigue. You have to become accustomed to discomfort to go to the next level.

- Creating the right environment is key to your success; give your workers or team members a good atmosphere, and they will thrive.

- Everyone needs to focus on their job for your workplace to be harmonious.

# A Photographer Who Can't Focus Is One Thing. A Beekeeper Who Can't Focus? Yikes!

As a photographer, I learned a long time ago that if I didn't figure out how to focus, I wasn't going to get very far in my career. Of course, understanding how to focus my camera was essential literally. Still, I also had to develop the ability to frame objects in my mind, set up a shot, gauge the light, and so much more. There are a million things that require adequate time and attention. Focusing both literally and figuratively can make or break a photograph.

When it comes to beekeeping, the stakes are considerably higher. If you aren't paying attention to the task at hand, you run the risk of losing your hive—or worse, severely injuring yourself. Honeybees are more than willing to sacrifice their own lives to protect the hive, and while one honeybee sting is painful, multiple honeybee stings can be life-threatening.

This can be applied to other aspects of life as well. There's a wide range of outcomes when you miss a photo or get stung by hundreds of honeybees—but losing focus is never helpful. In my experience as an entrepreneur, author, consultant, and beekeeper,

I've identified three main reasons people tend to lose focus, and I've also come up with numerous ways over the years on how to avoid them.

## They get lost in the big ideas

As CEOs and entrepreneurs, we tend to think big. We're the "big idea" people—our inspirations and passions are what got us started in the first place. But believe it or not, sometimes our big ideas can *get in the way* of our business. It's a textbook example of the phrase, "lose sight of the forest for the trees." The task at hand must be your priority, yes, long-term ambitions are significant, but short-term progress is even more critical. Think of it in terms of a small-scale example. We all knew a student back in our college years who decided to read up on a topic before the lecture. The student then decides he wants to learn more about the subject than what the course outlines entails and decides to read up on advanced stuff that he cannot yet understand completely. The next day, while attending the lecture, he constantly thinks about what he read earlier, and instead of asking relevant questions, he proceeds to ask the big questions. This may divert the course of the original lecture, confusing the student and his peers.

With entrepreneurs and newly budding businesses, we often tend to be overly ambitious and optimistic. Sure, there is no problem with dreaming. I highly encourage it. Those who fear to dream limit their ability to achieve greatness. That said, daydreaming can cause you to lose sight of the reality around you, which may directly affect your capacity as a leader as, at the end of the day, whatever you do impacts the general population. If you get too involved in your ideas and lose touch with reality, you may find it hard to relate or understand the problems of those under you who are directly affected by your ideas. This has moral implications, which in your capacity as a leader, must not be compromised.

I know this from experience. In the early days of Photos in a Minute, I was approached to bring our "Santa Photos" program to multiple stadiums throughout North America. At the time, it seemed like a fantastic opportunity to scale up significantly and immediately, so naturally, I got excited. When I started my business, it was my vision to provide that Santa experience to as many people as possible and make a considerable profit. As far as I could tell, my chance had just arrived.

I decided to do whatever it took to launch my big idea, but in my haste, I failed to work up one of my most important tools: a profitability chart. Today, I have a special process and software to pinpoint the profitability chart on every client before I even enter a bid, and certainly before we do a job. The chart details all the projected expenses and revenue (including a 5 percent margin for my mess-ups), then automatically figures out our likely profitability.

Back when I had this big idea of growing exponentially overnight, the excitement got to me. However, I didn't take the time to think beyond the *positive* numbers.

When you're a company of one and make a mistake, you might lose two or three thousand dollars. That's a lot of money, and nobody *wants* to lose that much. However, you have to survive and move on. This can't be applied in the later stages because when you scale up, the losses grow. The bigger you get, the more every mistake will cost you. When you grow from a small company to a larger company *overnight*, the losses can be enormous. That's what happened to me.

I was so focused on launching that. I didn't find out until it was too late. We needed to get all the equipment from our office in Massachusetts to Seattle for an event in forty-eight hours. I don't know if you've ever seen a Santa photo shoot, but there's a *lot* of heavy, delicate equipment involved. Due to the weight of the gear and the tight timeline, shipping costs ended up being exorbitant. That avoidable expense took a massive bite out of our profits, and it happened because I didn't plan accordingly.

That was only one of several mistakes made as I tried to scale up with little planning and little time. The schedule and disorganization of the project meant our small team was stretched beyond our capacity; everyone had to wear multiple hats. As I've since learned from the honeybees (and Bill Belichick), companies work best when every worker is allowed to focus on his or her job. When we tried to grow our business too fast, our worker bees tried to do more than they were hired to do. No one was focusing on their main task because we were all hustling to realize the big idea—*my* big idea.

Warren Buffett has been known to say he made more money by saying no than saying yes. It's a common refrain in the business world—you need to know when to turn down specific "opportunities" because although they may look good on paper, they'll end up costing you in the long run.

I share this story as a cautionary tale because it taught me a valuable lesson. When you're so focused on the grandness of an idea, you might start sacrificing the details. You run the risk of making costly or even fatal mistakes. I was lucky because I was able to recover. Not every business is so fortunate. Being celebrated for reaching the stars while having your rocket fall apart and causing destruction elsewhere hardly counts as the successful execution of an idea. The end goal surely matters, but the details that bring it to fruition matter more.

Understanding what's really needed for your big idea to materialize and what's not will make all the difference between success and failure. There's always the dream of larger profits when you think about growth. Fifty beehives are going to yield fifty times the honey, right? That tends to be what entrepreneurs focus on because we're dreamers and enthusiasts. I know because I'm one of them!

It's important to take a moment to focus on the *reality* of your dream because that reality also means an increase in cost and time. You have to scale up your whole operation, and that means more hives, more beekeepers, more equipment to collect honey, more vehicles to move the honey, more employees to sell the honey, more advertising to market the honey, and so on. There are always increased costs to growth. Only in time do these costs start to pay back in greater profit.

Do you have a retail store but are thinking of opening ten

more locations? Whatever the cost of your business is now, multiply it by ten. You're going to need ten times the number of registers, ten times the number of point-of-sale systems, and, depending on the size of your stores, at least ten times the staff. You'll also be paying ten times the amount in rent or mortgages and so on.

Can you also multiply your profit by ten? Maybe. However, that is far from a certainty. Maybe your profit will increase by *thirty*. Maybe it'll decrease *tenfold*. You can't say with absolute certainty. Profits can be expected but not guaranteed, so you should not lose faith and continue to dream big! Remember, depending on what new locations you're opening, it's possible. You should continue to dream big, but you can't count on that increase, so you have to put a good profitability chart and contingency plan in place. Of course, the big idea is appealing, but make sure you're just as focused on the logistics, or you're going to get stung.

You also have to consider how the change will affect your worker bees. Your big idea might involve new tasks that will require additional staff and positions. However, ask yourself these questions; do you have the appropriate human resource and payroll people in place for more employees? Are you confident you won't be asking your staff to split their focus? Will your honeybees have to work overtime to compensate for the load?

An actual worker bee doesn't have a long-term vision as far as we know, of course. She might not even have a concept of the hive as a whole. She's focused solely on her job, with an innate

" The big idea is appealing, but make sure you're just as focused on the logistics, or you're going to get stung. "

understanding that all the other honeybees around her are also focused on their jobs. She instinctively knows that if they all work together, they'll survive.

People are far more complex than honeybees, with a range of motivations, loyalties, and ambitions, but it's better not to assume your workers are as inspired and impassioned by your idea as you are. They might not have a personal stake in your growth as a company, but as long as they're doing great work, that's all right. Make sure you're giving them a chance to focus on what they do best, not stretching their capacity or diverting their focus. People are always limited in their understanding and capabilities. It is your job to figure those out as accurately and soon as possible, then apply them to your company.

## They don't focus on timing

For honeybees, *timing* is everything. They have an internal sense of the seasons—of when to forage and when to hibernate. In the summer, they work as hard as possible to gather as much food as possible. In winters, they make sure to consume as little energy to stay alive and make it through to the following summer. They've evolved over millions of years to hone their sense of timing and survive whatever comes their way.

For many people like me, our businesses are similarly seasonal. There are months when we're busy and months when we're slow. For companies like ours, cash flow is directly tied to those patterns. This is similar to how the "honey flow" can be expected in the beehive twice a year. For example, at Photos in a Minute, one of our specialties was Santa Claus photos with kids and family during the Christmas season. In the spring, after our photography session at the White House for the historical Easter Egg Roll during President Obama's presidencies, we began providing Easter bunny photos for the public as well. This brought our second "honey flow" up to twice a year. Our profits for the earning during these seasons began to grow exponentially.

For many seasonal businesses, busy times aren't tied to a specific date like Christmas or Easter, but they still have a general season. At Headshots in a Minute, we take corporate headshots—and while there's no specific day dictating the beginning of "headshot season," most companies aren't thinking about it in July. We find corporate America to be more in the mood for capturing headshots in September and October. This is around the same time kids are getting their school pictures taken. The Headshots in a Minute honey flow is in the fall, while those slow corporate summer months are better for foraging.

So, what does it mean for us to forage?

For human beings, foraging means preparation and pitching—also known as marketing. For example, if you know you're going to take fifty thousand Santa Claus photos in November and December, you don't want to wait until October to start lining up venues, equipment, and talent. Events like these take months of preparation. There are so many factors for us to juggle, and planning a new event, especially something you've never done before, takes even longer.

We pivoted our business during the global pandemic of

COVID-19. In 2020 and 2021, I used my downtime to forage new ideas, new clients, and perform market research to be innovative and focus on the future. What our business was pre-COVID will be much different post-COVID. I took that time to rest and plan a new way to rebuild our business slowly, just as honeybees will build painstakingly, layer by layer, to create a robust, thriving hive.

Of course, some things can't be predicted with total accuracy. A honeybee might launch from the hive on a beautiful day to go foraging, but not everything goes according to plan, and if the weather turns bad, it might not come back. Winter might be extra long one year, or a regional drought might make the flowers sparse. A sense of timing is essential, which is why honeybees also know how to plan for the unforeseen. The innate animal instinct helps them keep extra honey in reserve for emergencies like those.

As a beekeeper, you need to know how much honey you can take from the hive without causing a collapse in the winter. This collapse can also be seen in the wild, where hives tend to lose productivity due to several factors, mostly due to the unavailability of honeybees due to loss of habitat from human interference, or pathogens that infect the honeybees. Similarly, a CEO needs to be monitoring cash flow. Just like the beekeeper who takes honey out of the hive to sell, you can also take some of your money out to invest in new opportunities, pay your employees, and keep up to date with equipment and technology. The key here is *some* of your money, not all of it. Understanding the formula for your particular company can make the difference between merely surviving and thriving.

Timing is essential for a business of any sort, whether your product is seasonal or not. You need to read more than just the weather. Your ability to read the trends of the markets, new revenue streams, and advancements in technology will all affect the success of your business. This is what's often referred to as keeping your finger on the pulse. The times are constantly changing, and the key to being successful and maintaining a level of success is adapting. Honeybees might have this all down instinctually, but we humans have to put in the work to understand what makes good timing.

I often tell my team members and clients, "If you can anticipate you have a problem, you don't have one." Because you can plan accordingly, you'll make sure that plan is resolved before it is even birthed in the first place. If I know I'm going to have traffic on the way to the airport; I turn it into an opportunity. I leave four hours early, bring my Kindle, and grab a nice cup of coffee. I'm avoiding the traffic altogether and also catching up on reading. Problem solved.

If you could have ever anticipated that a particular virus outbreak would turn into a global pandemic, you'll probably update your business model and plan accordingly. Anyone who has been able to thrive and be successful in the COVID-19 era has done so because of their brilliant ability to adapt to the circumstances.

For honeybees, anticipating the changes in the weather is half the battle concerning the damage control that they can

" **What our business was pre-COVID will be much different post-COVID. I took that time to rest and plan a new way to rebuild our business slowly, just as honeybees will build paintakingly, layer by layer, to create a robust, thriving hive.** "

do. If you know you're going to have a bad winter, you can predict you won't have a good honey flow in the spring and plan accordingly. It may not be the outcome you were hoping for, but if you plan for it, it's not a problem.

When I worked at the White House, Michelle Obama started a massive beekeeping operation in the Rose Garden—a first for a First Lady. At the time, I'd just begun beekeeping, and I was intrigued by the size of the beehive that she had built. I had never seen anything like it before. My brand-new hobby hive was so small by comparison, and seeing this vast, sprawling honeybee habitat really sparked my imagination.

Of course, I didn't have the resources that Michelle Obama had at the White House, so building my honeybee business to the same degree wasn't really an option—unless I quit my job, invested everything I had, and went into beekeeping full time. That seemed ill-advised for various reasons, not the least of which was that beekeeping was supposed to be a fun distraction—something that helped me take my focus *off* of work—not my full-time business.

As usual, it wasn't an either/or proposition. There were many options between my small hive operation and the giant system in place at the White House. It was simply a matter of deciding how much I wanted to grow.

I recently coached a client, Pedro Lopez (for his privacy, that name is made up). He runs a small and very successful family-owned landscaping business. I've been helping him and

**66** **Your ability to read the trends of the markets, new revenue streams, and advancements in technology will all affect the success of your business.** **99**

his brother make decisions and serve his own clientele for years. During our call, I could tell he was distracted, so finally, I asked him what was up.

"Scott," he said, sounding almost nervous, "What do you think about us not growing?"

It was an unusual question from a client—usually, I hear the opposite. I thought about it for a minute and said, "That depends. How do you feel about not growing?"

He sighed. "I don't know if I want this business to get any bigger."

"Why?"

"I feel like there's all this pressure from society that I should want to grow. But I really like the size we are now."

That was the answer I was hoping to hear.

"Well," I said. "You definitely don't have to grow. In fact, if you don't really want to, I would say it's not a good idea."

As his coach, I needed to find out why he didn't want to grow before I knew how to advise him properly. After all, I can't tell him to do something he shouldn't. So after hearing his explanation, I understood his mindset, motives, and insecurities better. Suppose the reason was about fear or discomfort with complexity that I talked about in Chapter 1. In that case, I might have encouraged him to sit with the idea for a while, maybe do a profitability chart and reconnect with the big idea behind his business.

66 **Anyone who has been able to thrive and be successful in the COVID-19 era has done so because of their brilliant ability to adapt to the circumstances.** 99

However, his hesitancy to grow had nothing to do with fear or discomfort. In fact, it was the opposite in his case—he was uncomfortable at the prospect of not wanting to grow. So, I felt fine affirming his instinct to keep his business where it was. I didn't encourage him to apply for business loans, buy more equipment, or add trucks to his company just for the sake of doing so. If he didn't want to grow, why should he? Especially when he's already successful, there doesn't seem to be a demand for him to expand.

We can get distracted by the *idea* of growth, and sometimes it doesn't even feel like our own idea. Just like my client said, society can make you feel like something is wrong if you're not constantly dreaming of being the biggest on the block. As we've already seen, to keep scaling up means a lot more work and investment. It's up to you to decide what you want to focus on and what you don't. Suppose you feel like you're providing the best customer service at your current level. In that case, you probably don't want to be removed entirely from the day-to-day business, so your corporation runs smoothly. If you're already living the life you want to live, there's no reason to focus on growth. You have to focus on yourself and what you want.

Rather than make the goal of unending growth, I encourage my clients to identify where they want to end up, then work backward from there. This is a different and unique approach but works wonders if you have the end goal in mind. If you decide you want to open four restaurants, you'll feel a tremendous sense of accomplishment when you cut the ribbon on the fourth. Only you know your resources, capacity, and dreams, so you are the only person who can set a realistic goal for yourself with a pragmatic timeline that you believe you can follow. The first person you need to sell your idea to is you. If you can't do that, you will not be able to sell it to anyone else. There's always an opportunity to adjust that goal once it's been reached. Let's assume you've opened four restaurants and realize you still want to grow. Reset your plan for ten, or refocus your energy on expanding into new geographic areas. Now you've set yourself up for more success, and you can measure your goals accordingly.

Maybe your goal has nothing to do with size. Perhaps you want to concentrate on making customer service second to none. Maybe your goal is to be rated the best employer by increasing employee benefits and loyalty. Maybe your goal is to have the highest-quality product, so you're focused on improving on that. You can think outside of the box when setting goals. It doesn't have to be just about your profit margins. It may be hard to believe, but positive growth extends beyond monetary profits. It can exist in many other forms as well.

If you don't have a goal, it's harder to define success and easier to get caught up in a web of comparison which is why I always advise you to thoroughly ponder over your goals. You must understand where you are headed and where you want to go, so you can create a road map to get there. Measuring yourself against other businesses is one of the most dangerous and counterproductive things you can waste your time on. Every business is different, and the people running them are different as well. You don't know where those other businesses started, what's happening in their books, or what they've sacrificed to get where they are. If you were to open up their hive, you might not like what you see in there. You just never know.

My advice is to figure out where you're coming from and where you're going. Never compare yourself with others. Only compare yourself with your past and your future selves. That way, you'll have a more accurate reflection of your successes.

66 **You can think outside of the box when setting goals. It doesn't have to be just about your profit margins. It may be hard to believe, but positive growth extends beyond monetary profits. It can exist in many other forms as well.** 99

# 🐝 Buzzing Points

As you identify your priorities and decide what to focus on, here's what to keep in mind:

- Don't focus too much on your big idea. The devil is in the details. It's okay to have a brief outline or direction of what the future holds, not an accurate blueprint description.

- Use a profitability chart and other tools to make sure you're not too focused on your big idea at the expense of those details of your business.

- Scaling up your operation means scaling up your costs and asking more of your team. Are you prepared to do that? Can you deal with the expected consequences?

- Consider how your big idea will affect your whole team. Will they be able to continue doing what they do with the same level of excellence, or will they have to wear multiple hats, which may pull them away from their core tasks?

- If you're too focused on the big idea and not enough on the logistics, you run the risk of making significant mistakes.

- Respect the seasonal trends that affect your business. Use slower months to plan and market, knowing you'll be too busy during your "honey flow" seasons.

- You can't predict everything, so maintain emergency reserves and plans for rainy days.

- Anticipating problems is solving problems.

- Consider what it means to grow before you decide you want to. Remember, you don't have to grow. If you're happy where you are, focus on improving what you want to improve.

- Identify a goal and work backward from there.

- Don't compare your business to other businesses.

# Bees Do Their Jobs . . .
# So Why Don't People Do Theirs?

There is never any confusion in a beehive when it comes to completing tasks and fulfilling responsibilities. We already know about their extraordinary dedication to work. Each honeybee knows what to do and does it the best she can, without question. The loyalty and devotion that a honeybee provides to its hive are truly unparalleled. If only people were so consistent!

You can never see a honeybee giving its "fifty" percent to work. She is always going to put her hundred percent effort into everything. If a task needs to be carried out, she would prioritize its completion above everything else and immediately get started with her job. Due to their tremendous commitment to work, honeybees always stand out from other insects. They primarily focus on making their community incredibly efficient and are experts in their work; this benefits them in work and helps them promote a harmonious bond between all hive members, which is rarely seen in human society today.

The truth is, we humans treasure our individuality and personal talents for good reason: we want people who bring unique abilities and personalities to their jobs. This is what keeps life exciting and makes each business special! If everyone showed up wearing the same outfit, with the same goals and the same mindset, the office would not be a fun place to work anymore; the real charm lies in diversity. Remember that your people are your business, so it's crucial you find and keep the right people for the right jobs.

We have all been gifted in different ways; just like honeybees, we all possess different traits, qualities, habits, and work styles. Some of us have good time management skills or research skills, whereas others have a tremendous work ethic. Therefore, while choosing your employees, you need to be sure of hiring the right fit for the position. You cannot simply expect a carpenter to do a plumbing job, can you?

Up until now, we have been becoming aware of the operations carried out by the honeybees. Now, let's take a look at how we can use it to achieve our business goals and also to run your company as efficiently as a beehive.

## If you're the CEO, you're the queen bee

Most people know a beehive has only one queen—"the mother" of every honeybee in the hive. A lesser-known but equally fascinating fact is that the queen mates just once in her life. After that one mating excursion, she settles in the hive and lays thousands of eggs, season after season, for up to seven years.

According to researchers, honeybees and flowers communicate with one another, just like humans. A study was conducted at the University of Bristol, which found that honeybees were in a lot of ways similar to humans. They can easily detect and "read" the positive and negative charge of plants. The bees' reactive positive charge tends to react with the electrical field of the plants and changes their charge for several minutes after producing their nectar and collecting their pollens. This whole process reflects their smartness; this task is carried out only so that the other honeybees can avoid the affected plants until the flower regenerates its nectar and other resources.

According to Professor Daniel Robert: *"The last thing a flower wants is to attract a honeybee and then fail to provide nectar; a lesson in honest advertising since honeybees are good learners and would soon lose interest in such unrewarding flower."* This certainly means that queen bees are only interested in taking out work from their resources, otherwise, those means become useless to them, and they quickly lose their interest.

While we as people definitely don't do the same literally, like a queen bee, a CEO usually becomes "impregnated" with a great idea once. They then launch a company with the same passion, energy, and labor it takes to birth thousands of eggs. The CEO provides the plans and materials that ensure the health and success of the hive, spending the bulk of their time laying down the groundwork. Everyone else on the team feeds off the CEO's energy; the company is only as effective as each person is in their role. Like the queen bee, the CEO of any company gives the right direction to achieve the goal. They provide their team with the energy, power, and motivation that's needed to reach the objective. Without the presence of a queen bee, the hive might become a mess. All that background work, prediction, and vision are needed to prevent future losses and any disturbance during their work.

The queen bee teaches the CEOs that they need to represent their personal power, strength, and abilities in their decisions and always take a stand for their employees when needed. The sweetness of honey can be compared to the joy and satisfaction of reaching your business goals. In contrast, the failure of extracting nectar from any flower could relate to the idea of not achieving any business objective. The queen bee strongly represents the complex relationship between your targets and your accomplishments, too; she keeps track of the nectar gathered throughout the day and the job of each resource that helped produce such a large quantity of flower juice.

One of your best assets for not only surviving but thriving is surrounding yourself with the right workers. Basically, this kind of worker knows how to take ownership of their work, which really adds up to the progress and growth of the company. Hiring the right person means that you are indirectly putting the relevant energy into the right place. It helps you carry out the tasks efficiently and saves a lot of your time and energy that you need to invest in their training.

Once you have your perfect team in place, you have already achieved half of your goal. Now, the next step is to set the tone and culture from the top down; set the direction of the work carefully. The initial years are always very crucial for a company as they play a major role in setting the norms and values at your workplace. Like I mentioned earlier, you are the only person responsible for improving the work environment of your company. So, never refrain from taking the lead; you need to give your administrative team the full operational rights and be aware of the ongoing operations, tasks, and consequences of every decision.

## Teamwork is the goal and a process

Just as building a company is a process, so is building a hive. The first step is to buy the hive kit. It comes with a lot of different parts, so you need to understand the purpose and application of each component. Then you have to figure out how all the pieces fit together and decide the best place to put it. You don't simply put a hive next to your home, or else you'll suffer for as long as the hive exists. You need to find a sheltered and isolated spot that isn't easily accessible to people and animals. Both are dangerous creatures that intentionally or unintentionally provoke honeybees (and, of course, they face the consequences of any provocation, as well).

Then you have to find a queen bee and populate the hive with workers. I have described that exhilarating bit in detail in Chapter 1. However, the point is that setting up a beehive is similar to buying or starting a company. You have to first rent an office space, figure out what you need to furnish it with, and hire a team to work in it. It sounds simple, but those who have done it know it's far from that.

Similarly, while setting up your business, you need to make sure you are taking care of each and every little step to establish your company. From choosing the right place to hiring the relevant people, you need to align every task with your objective. Like a hive, a business is built layer by layer, one step at a time— and even though you are the one with the ideas and the passion, you always do it alone. Trust me when I tell you, no amount of passion and perseverance will get you to the top if you don't work with others. You have to put your trust in others for them to put their's in you.

You need to realize the significance of team making. No organization in this whole world can run through a "one-man" show. No matter how efficient, productive, or multi-talented you are, you need to distribute the responsibility of each team member according to their experience, skills, and expertise.

This idea can be compared to the concept of bees' hive operations again. No queen bee survives on her own. She needs to have worker bees to support her. The best businesses are full of people committed and enthusiastic about an idea and focused on their part in bringing that idea to fruition. The only key is that you all work together to achieve a collective goal and keep the company's objective in your mind.

"But Scott, I bought a fully functioning company, already up and running for years," you might be thinking. "I don't have to put it together layer by layer from the ground up. I just have to step in and be in charge, right?"

Well, not exactly. We can still learn from the honeybees in this instance. When you bring a queen bee into a hive, she has to be "introduced." The workers must dig to find her, all the while

" Trust me when I tell you, no amount of passion and perseverance will get you to the top if you don't work with others. You have to put your trust in others for them to put their's in you. "

getting used to her scent and acclimating to the change in their environment. Taking over an existing company is similar for a new CEO. The team you're leading already has its own work habits and communication mode. You'll need to first understand how they work and adjust to their work lifestyle. Similarly, you'll need to give them time to adjust to your leadership and your vision for the company.

You cannot simply expect those hundreds or thousands of employees to transform their work habits within a day. Neither can you "force" them to start following your rules and regulations overnight. Instead, you need to wait for some weeks or maybe months to implement a new policy. Your first step should always be to observe and get observed by the employees so they become well-adjusted to your ideas behind work. The initial few months should be spent analyzing each and every small detail of the company. Remember, this observational phase will never come back; you need to be extremely alert to monitor and supervise everything. From the cleaning conditions of your company to the yearly profits, you need to be well-aware and informed about each and every detail.

I am going to mention Tom Brady again, so forgive me if you're not a New England Patriots fan (or perhaps a Tampa Bay fan). Whether you love him or hate him, we can all agree he's a remarkable talent, one of the greatest who has ever played. There's no way the Patriots would have won as many Super Bowls as they have without Tom Brady, and everyone knows that.

But here's the thing: Tom Brady has not won those Super Bowls without the rest of the team. Football isn't played by one person but rather by a team. The forward, mid-field, and defenders all combine to form one cohesive unit. The Tampa Bay Buccaneers isn't a team of eleven Tom Brady's but rather ten distinct and talented people working alongside Tom to represent their team and succeed. Yes, he was the star and the leader, and he shouldered much of the responsibility, but he still needed the entire team backing him up and playing its absolute best, each member performing his job, for things to go right.

Also, you need to understand what it means to be part of a team in an office. As CEO, you might draw the lion's share of the spotlight. That's not always positive fame and glory. In heated situations, you will have to withstand a lot of heat as well. Maybe you have a killer salesperson who dominates every quarter or a star designer in an idea factory. There will always be standouts. However, a solid, hardworking *group* of people is still essential to the overall success of your business. It is important to celebrate hard work, not just that of the stars who shine the brightest. Remember, the result usually comes from the team effort, not a singular worker.

## Focusing on your Top Three Wins

So, what happens when a promising, motivated worker is simply not focused on his/her job? Not long ago, I had this issue with one of my team members. She was a hard worker—conscientious and enthusiastic. The rest of the team liked her as well, so it was especially difficult when it became clear there was a problem. Somehow, even though she was trying, she wasn't getting her work done.

As I looked more closely at the problem, I found that I was unsurprisingly at the center of it. In this particular case, I was communicating too much. Sometimes my mind works too fast, and I tend to get ahead of myself. That energy influenced her as well. She was susceptible to my enthusiasm, but she was also easily distracted when I overshare the plans for the future. I involved her in challenging areas that didn't concern her, and she started to bear the burden of the overall narrative of the company alongside me. I communicated too much essential information, making it harder for her to concentrate on her one job. That was the point when I realized not everyone could process tons of information at once.

After that, I became more aware of what information I was burdening her with and encouraged her instead to refocus every day on her Top Three Wins. This is a method I learned to stay focused and productive whenever I'm feeling distracted and overwhelmed. I love asking kids this same question. "What were your three wins for the day?" It's amazing the answers I get back. I learned from asking kids these questions for years because they don't need to be big wins, which makes me appreciate as a win something as simple as a perfectly brewed coffee at three o'clock (join me at www.3OclockCoffeePodcast.com)

Kids used to give answers like, "I painted a toy car," "I brushed my teeth by myself in the morning," or "I saw a frog today." I realized we all need constant encouragement and motivation in our lives. From time to time, we need to take a look at our accomplishments or wins for the day to keep our focus on the goals and never get distracted.

Many people recommend keeping a running to-do list, and it's an important tool I use. However, if you're anything like me, your comprehensive to-do list can have twenty or thirty items on it. Sometimes, reviewing everything you have on your plate can have the opposite of the desired effect—it can make you feel even more overwhelmed. For example, your whole-day list could include all your work activities, morning routine, gym hours, diet and health rituals, regular meetings, or doctor appointments. Although it can greatly help you to plan your day in a much better way, it still makes some people uncomfortable; the idea of handling so many tasks in a single day might get on nerves.

That's why every morning, I write down the top three goals I want to accomplish that day. Then, whenever I find myself off in the weeds, I return to that shortlist. Keeping the list of your short-term goals simple and precise makes it easier to accomplish them. It makes the tasks more digestible and less intimidating, which are two of the biggest hurdles in slowing down progress. Three is a manageable, realistic number of goals, and if I can accomplish those three goals for the day, I can go home and say, "I did something today." I feel accomplished knowing it was a productive day, and I feel closer to my honeybees as they work day in and day out for their hive. I use this method to help my team or coaching clients refocus if they've lost the thread of where they're supposed to be. It helps a lot of people in my social circle to get back on track.

66 I write down the top three goals I want to accomplish that day. Then, whenever I find myself off in the weeds, I return to that shortlist. Keeping the list of your short-term goals simple and precise makes it easier to accomplish them. 99

## The right people in the right place

Building your team is all about finding the right people. In a beehive, there's no concern about hiring the "right" honeybees—they're born to do their work and take to it instinctually. The workers fetch the pollen, and the drones mate with the queen, the queen lays her eggs . . . there's no confusion or question of suitability for their roles. After all, there aren't many roles.

The skill sets and temperaments needed in a business might be harder to identify, as the roles are so diverse and unique. Some are so interlinked that they need regular synchronization. In contrast, others are completely unrelated and have nothing to do with each other. However, it's just as important to have the right workers in the correct positions of a company as it is in a hive. In my books *Camera Focus* and *The Big Picture*, I talk about using the Kolbe Index™. This aptitude test helps identify a person's natural strengths and weaknesses. It analyzes personalities to see which of the four Action Modes a person most fits into—Fact Finder, Follow Thru, Quick Start, or Implementor.

A tool like the Kolbe Index™ is effective only if you use it the right way. Here's the key: Don't look for people with the overall highest scores. If you're looking to fill a particular role, you don't need someone to be totally well-rounded. The goal isn't to find people who score the highest in general but the highest in the most relevant skills for the job in question.

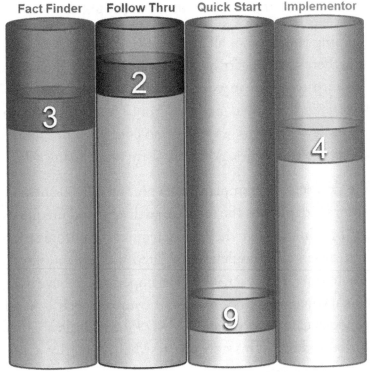

Fact Finder  Follow Thru  Quick Start  Implementor

Think of it this way. You need the best offensive player for your team to be in the front lines instead of an all-rounder who's just okay at everything. Yes, he can help many others, but a Jack of all trades is often a master of none. Your team should be a well-oiled machine of workers who are all great at what they do. Everyone has their respective specialties that help bring the best output possible.

I'm definitely the Quick Starter on our team. Like most CEOs, I have big ideas, make decisions quickly, and am enthusiastic about trying the "next big thing." It's a very important quality for a CEO to have. But an office full of Quick Starters? That would be rather dysfunctional.

Building a workplace atmosphere that encourages creativity and innovation has always been a challenging task. However, it's extremely important for the company's progress and especially for its growth. I believe that choosing skilled and experienced people for the relevant fields is always beneficial for both parties. This way, you get to realize the true potential of your employee and also benefit from their abilities. For instance, if you are an accountant, how would you feel if any company asked you to work as a graphic designer? The answer is obvious; you would definitely refuse because you do not have anything to offer in that field. Similarly, being the CEO it is essential for you to do the relevant hiring so each role is carried out efficiently and productively.

Each position has its own specific need. You probably want your quality control person to be a decent Fact Finder, your human resources manager to be a good Implementor, your project manager to fall under the Follow Thru umbrella, and so on. Some roles may benefit from more than one strength, but not everyone has to score high all around. What's important is finding the right tool to help you identify the exact qualities you're looking for and the person who possesses those qualities. Merely having those qualities isn't enough; you need to look for an employee who can practically implement the work and get their hands on the task. That is the reason why degrees do not work everywhere! The practical demonstration is necessary to know what skills you possess.

## Communication is key

It would not be wrong to say that communication is the "most important" part of every business. Without it, you can never run a company. As I mentioned before, honeybees have a very set system of communication. They keep the whole team informed about their ongoing operations, tasks, and progress. In a hive, honeybees have a very intricate system of communicating with each other. They use movements often referred to as "dancing." Bees have a language that allows them to communicate the location of and distance to promising food supplies. They also use pheromones to communicate odors, health status, and warnings of possible danger. It's a complex, detailed system that has developed and evolved over millennia.

As a business beekeeper, I can't speak the instinctual language of my honeybees, no matter how hard I try. Still, as their coach, I need a mode of communication to make sure we all stay productive and safe when working together.

Smoke is one of the tools beekeepers use to send messages to the honeybees. When it's time to collect honey, we use a process called "smoking the hive." I personally can't emit a pheromone that will tell the honeybees what's going on. Still, when they smell smoke, it seems to have a calming or sedating effect on them. This is critical as it helps them move to the bottom of the hive, allowing me to reach in and collect the honey. Otherwise, it would be an intense death battle between the honeybees and the beekeeper because the honeybees would be more than furious about having to give up the precious nectar they've worked all day every day to collect.

This communication protects me from honeybee stings, but it also protects the honeybees. A honeybee has but one sting to give. If one honeybee stings me because I haven't adequately communicated my intentions, it will die. In that way, our fates are tied together. It benefits us all to proceed calmly.

As a CEO, you also need to occasionally "smoke the hive." While literal smoke doesn't have a calming effect on humans, clear, concise, and honest information does. It's important to keep open a consistent line of communication at all times, periodically checking in with your people and making sure they know they can bring thoughts, concerns, and ideas to you. The most important thing is to have mutual trust. When there's change or uncertainty, the whole team looks to you as CEO to listen to them and share your plan for moving forward. They look up to you, and you need to live up to that level of trust.

Of course, that doesn't mean you always have to share every detail, motivation, or projected outcome. As I mentioned earlier, too much information can have a detrimental effect, causing people to worry and distracting them from their jobs. There exists a delicate equilibrium between necessary information and too much context. Suppose you want to be a good CEO. In that case, you need to find that delicate balance between constructive communication and the lack thereof. You also need to keep your people on the essential task to your team's morale and efficiency. Just like with the honeybees, your fates are tied to your mutual success. I want my team members to be happy and hardworking, and they want the business to succeed—or else they'll be out of work. It's a win-win.

You can never ensure your business's smooth and efficient functioning unless you have an effective and robust communication system with your workers. Being the CEO, you need to make sure you are not encouraging any communication gap between you and your employees. It can harm your overall progress. In some cases, people can really benefit from your lack of interaction too. For example, spreading wrong information to their subordinates, taking false credits for someone else's work, etc. Frequent communication will provide you with the exact details on every employee's progress and also the effort they are putting in to their everyday work. This is a necessary tool for direction and leadership as it has the power to align people with the company goals and desires of the management.

## Finding the proper modes of communication

An odd fact is that the queen bee and many worker bees never leave their immediate surroundings. They spend their whole lives inside the hive, busily working for its success. Then there are the foragers, who venture out into the world to find sustenance and bring it back to the hive. They use their special communication skills to let the other honeybees know what they've learned on the outside.

I've said many times that, as the CEO, you're the queen of your hive. However, you'll also need to take a lesson from the honeybees who forage for sustenance when it comes to communication. When you're inside, you're in charge, and you'll want to develop a clear, consistent language to communicate with your team. However, there will be instances from time to time where you'll also need to venture out into the world and bring back valuable information. You can't simply do that from the inside.

If I've learned anything from my three o'clock coffee habit, it's that you have to push yourself beyond your comfortable boundaries. The phrase comfort zone is used precisely for this reason. You need to break out of your comfort zone and adapt to uncertain circumstances. They are often unfavorable and even challenging, but nothing good is ever achieved without difficulties.

When I started contacting CEOs of multimillion-dollar companies to see if they'd have a coffee with me, it was a leap of faith. Some people didn't seem interested, but on the whole, you'd be amazed at how accessible and generous people can be when you reach out with no hidden agenda.

The most effective business people are those who are always their authentic selves. It doesn't matter who they're talking to; as long as they are themselves, it brings out an honest and valid opinion. Whether that's thousands of employees, a board of directors, or me, sitting across from them at a Caribou Coffee, transparency goes a long way toward establishing trust. Similarly, hypocrisy only gets you so far. If you're not passionate about what you do or don't believe in what you say, it will come back to bite you one day.

One person who exemplifies this principle is Peter

Diamandis. I met Peter a few years ago at a business workshop I attend each quarter. I learned more about communication by watching him interact with people. Peter is a billionaire mindset entrepreneur in the fields of longevity, space, venture capital, and education. He has started more than twenty companies, including BOLD Capital Partners, a venture fund with a $250 million investment in exponential technologies. He has degrees in molecular genetics and aerospace engineering from MIT and holds an MD from Harvard Medical School. He has spent his career communicating complex ideas to various audiences—from stakeholders and consumers to the many readers of his best-selling books.

I learned so much from spending the day with Peter. He has an aura about him, and it doesn't emerge from his title, wealth, or even his track record. What makes Peter genuinely remarkable to me is how he talks, thinks, and asks questions. In other words, it's all about how he communicates. He's focused, curious, and approachable, but he also doesn't waste time and energy on things that don't matter. At a certain point that day, I shifted my note-taking from focusing on the workshop to focus on what Peter was doing. I observed how he took notes, how he interacted with his assistants, what he found important. Just being in proximity to a billionaire, I learned a lot. I began to model his behavior and adopt his modes of communication into my lifestyle.

What I began to develop that day was something you'll hear many people talk about: company culture, which is just another way to describe how people within a company communicate.

I mean whether they use Zoom or Slack, but also what the communication is like in tone and frequency and how things are said nonverbally.

Like most other facets of a business, this standard is set from the top down. Your employees will watch how you communicate with everyone, from the student interns to the legacy team members to the CFO, and it will affect the company culture. Your workers will know if you're a different person when you speak to them and when you speak to investors, and it will affect the way they deal with you and each other. Just as you'll model modes of communication after the business people you admire most, your whole team will model its communication style after you, so think carefully about the culture you want to establish.

Of course, you can model yourself after someone you want to emulate, but you'll also want to tweak things to make them your own. You want to learn to be the best you, not the best copy of someone else. The best you can be is an amalgamation of all the people you look up to, adding to your unique personality. When I spent the day with Peter, I noticed he began many conversations with new people by asking, "What's your joy?" I really loved that as an icebreaker because it acknowledges that people have a life beyond their work or that, at the very least, the work they do brings them joy. In my own life, I've modified this to ask people I regularly see, "What's your one win for today?" It's a question that can apply to anyone, whether it's my team members, my nephew Matthew, or the checkout person at the supermarket. Asking people what their win is will engage them and allow them to reflect on something positive. That's what I want people to associate me with, in their minds—something positive.

Beyond setting the communication culture for your team, you also have to figure out the best ways to literally communicate with it. For this, there's no one-size-fits-all answer. Technology is always changing, and we're constantly adapting to better forms of communication. Plus, every person is different, and often various projects require different modes of communication. Some people on your team will want to just pick up the phone and call you to talk things out; others will like everything in writing, such as an email, so they can refer back to that email when they need guidance. Some projects will need to live in a shared space where people can edit a reshared documents. It all depends on the specifics of the moment and the people involved.

What's important is that you don't expect new software or a new platform to suddenly work perfectly for everyone. Asking everyone to learn a new tool won't necessarily make your life simpler. As the CEO, I've found it more effective to be flexible when communicating with my team—I've adapted to their needs rather than asking them to adapt to mine. Technology is meant to work for you, not the other way around. Suppose you find an inordinate amount of time going toward teaching your team to adapt to some new program or platform. In that case, you might want to reconsider whether it's worth the time and effort or if it's more of a distraction. It's a lot more convenient and efficient for one person to adapt than a whole company.

66 **Communication is your most valuable tool in the workplace. Your "company culture" is all about how you communicate with your team and how you encourage them to communicate with each other.** 99

**Buzzing Points**

Building your team, establishing a company culture, and maintaining a positive work environment will be central to your company's success. Here are the main things to keep in mind as you assemble the right people for the right jobs:

- The CEO is the queen bee, and the coach, and occasionally a forager too.

- Because your best bet for success is hiring the right people, use the Kolbe Index™ or another personality assessment tool.

- It doesn't matter if a person scores an overall high score on such a test. What is important is that he or she is the most appropriate person for the job in question.

- Communication is your most valuable tool in the workplace. Your "company culture" is all about how you communicate with your team and how you encourage them to communicate with each other.

- Keep that line of communication open and your team members in the loop so they know they can trust you.

- Your team is counting on you to set the tone and make plans for the future. Sometimes you have to "smoke the hive" and calm everyone down by sharing information and communicating those plans.

• On the flip side, make sure you're communicating the right amount of information with your team members. You don't want to overwhelm them.

• Adjust your communication style to mesh with your own personality and your company culture.

• Keep up on new modes of communication and model the behavior of CEOs you want to emulate.

• Draw any distracted team members (including yourself) back to a list of their "Top Three Wins"— three goals to accomplish that day.

• Be ready to venture out into the world and bring back information.

• Be your most authentic self, no matter whom you're talking to.

• Make technology work for you. Sometimes you have to be flexible and adapt to the needs of your team members rather than trying to find a one-size-fits-all solution.

# Why One Beehive Can't Have Two Queen Bees

One beehive can't have two queen bees. It is similar to the jungle, where there cannot be two alpha lions. I've said this before, but it bears repeating. The meat of this message lies deep and hidden in the realization of it. That is why it is imperative to let it flow through you more than once until you fully understand the gravity of it. It's such an important point and the kind of thing you can know intellectually but not truly understand until you've experienced the repercussions of getting it wrong. It is very similar to one of the things in your practical life, where you know certain things by the rule of thumb but do not take them seriously until you learn them the hard way. That idea inspired this whole book, so I'm going to tell you about how, even though I recognized this concept intellectually, I still had to learn it the hard way. Twice. What I am trying to tell you here is, do not repeat the same mistake I made while learning the concept I am trying to articulate.

The first time I learned it was with actual honeybees. I still remember that day clearly. Not only because of the invaluable lesson I learned but also because it caught me off-guard, and there was little I could do by that time. One day I was outside near my hives when there was a sudden swarm. I was going about with my day and following my regular routine—there was nothing extraordinary about it. But the sudden appearance of a swarm startled me. Confusion rushed through my mind as I began to wonder why all of a sudden? I searched for clues, and there were quite a few obvious ones indicating what could possibly have gone wrong. I assumed that a second queen must have hatched inside a hive, and half the worker bees must have followed her while bursting out of the hive like a tornado and swirling around in my backyard. I was about five feet away when it happened, and it sounded like a helicopter had taken off above me. Imagine the buzzing sound of bees but multiply in ten or even twenty thousand honeybees. Other than the loud buzzing noise of the honeybee swarming, the sight was equally incredible.

I knew there were safe ways to recapture a swarm, but because I hadn't had any warning, I wasn't prepared to do so. Had I seen the swarm from afar and while it was developing, I'd have run to get some tools and tackle the situation in a manner safest for me and the bees. However, when I saw that the rebellious honeybees latched onto a branch about fifty feet above me, well out of reach, there was nothing I could do. At that moment, I realized, and knew as well, that eventually, the swarm would drift into the woods and try to find another home in nature. Sadly, it also meant that my hive would be left at half capacity, with a diminished chance for survival. It was concerning for me, but I had no control over the situation at hand. So, I stood there as a spectator, watching these two factions of the aggravated swarm, fighting over the domination of a home and deciding who got to stay or leave. About a year later, I was inspecting my hives when I noticed something odd. Even though everything looked as normal as could be from the outside, the insides told a different story. There were several large peanut-shaped larvae that looked different from the other larvae in the hive. It came to me that this must be the result of cross-species breeding. After carefully examining the larvae, I knew right away I was looking at multiple queen bee eggs. I just stared for a moment at all the larvae of varying sizes and reached the conclusion I didn't want multiple queens hatching inside of one hive—I'd seen what that led to—but there they were. I could see right away this was going to be a problem, but I wasn't sure what to do. The problem might be days, if not weeks, away from now till these larvae eggs reached maturity. Still, I could sense an impending crisis waiting to occur within this hive. Then again, I was not in control of the situation and did not really know how to counter the looming mess that could erupt out of control at any time.

Well, I did what any good CEO or coach would do: I brought in a consultant. Since I was at my wit's end after analyzing the overall scenario and reaching a dead-end, bringing an expert seemed a better idea. My friend Marc Laplante is a local city council member and an avid beekeeper. He and his wife, Susan, came over to check out the situation. I called them because I knew that if anyone could help me out in this matter, it'd be Marc. Since he had a history of beekeeping, it occurred to me that, like me, he too must have encountered a similar situation. Therefore, he must know how to handle it. The three of us were looking at the larvae, trying to figure out a plan of action, when right in front of us, one of the queen bee eggs started to hatch.

We were absolutely amazed at what was happening. Seeing that tiny larva struggling out of its membranous, translucent, and flexible material covering that nurtured it for days was an exhilarating moment. I had known Marc for many years, and he knew of my history as a photographer for National Geographic as well. As I stood transfixed, hyper-focusing on this extraordinary feat of nature, he turned to me and said, "Aren't you going to take a photo?"

I thought about it for a moment, then quoted one of my favorite movies, *The Secret Life of Walter Mitty*, quote.

"Sometimes I don't. If I like a moment, for me, personally, I don't like to have the distraction of the camera. I just want to stay in it." It was one of those experiences where viewing the world through your eye's lens is a much profound experience than seeing the same through a camera's lens. I knew what I was seeing was remarkable, and I wanted to stay present—to "bee focused," so to speak.

It was a fascinating thing to watch. After seeing the baby bee getting out of the soft egg membrane, we snapped out of the moment and concentrated on the task at hand. But, we still knew two queen bees in one hive wasn't going to work. We were going to have to take action and swiftly, unlike the last time, when the second queen and ensuing swarm took me by surprise. The three of us had just one task to focus on—split the honeybees in a way so that each queen would get a fair share. Of course, unlike humans, this was a different ball game

> **66** Sometimes I don't. If I like a moment, for me, personally, I don't like to have the distraction of the camera. I just want to stay in it. **99**
>
> - The Secret Life of Walter Mitty, with Sean O'Connell

altogether. Still, it was worth taking a shot and doing our best. With Marc and Susan's help, we "split" the hive, moving the new queen and some worker bees to another honeybee hive in a controlled manner. Then it became a waiting game. The new queen bee had to leave her hive, mate, return to the hive, and start laying eggs. We did as per our plan to separate the two different colonies ruled by two different honeybees. The three of us had our hopes high, and we assumed that the split of hives would work. Mark seemed more optimistic and had a smile on his face after we successfully executed what we intended. He had a show of faith look on his face, and I could not tell if it was based on his beekeeping experience, or whether he believed in me doing what a CEO does the best. In any case, I'd set them up for success to the best of my ability; the rest was up to nature.

When I checked back about two weeks later, there was a whole crop of new larvae, and the transferred worker bees were being productive. The transfer had worked! I was more than happy to finally make the most of the situation—bringing Marc over, deciding, and splitting hives. It was one of those moments when you see your plan working and coming to fruition. However, all the development needed time to happen, and when it did, it brought joy to my face. Seeing the two honeybees doing their bee-thing their separate ways was a similar experience.

I've been telling this story since it happened years ago—it's one of my favorites. Not only does the message of the story indulge the listeners, but it also stresses the importance of it in a unique way. However, I almost always get the same questions in response after telling this tale: "How does the new queen know when it's time to leave the hive? And how do half the workers know to go with her?"

Well, the right answer to this question never occurred to me because I'm not a scientist—I'm sure an entomologist could provide a more accurate theory. However, I've settled on an answer I think makes the most sense in a layman's terms.

"They just know. They get a 'vibe.'" No, they can't talk about it, draw up contracts, or plot a takeover like humans do. However, honeybees have an instinct for these things that's just beyond our human sensibility. We can see it happen but cannot reason the logic of "it" happening in front of our eyes.

Or is it beyond our sensibility? On some level, many of us have experienced something similar to this vibe—it's something akin to a sixth sense, a premonition, and a strong pull in a particular direction. As I said, it is hard to put this thought into words. It takes birth and develops inside your head. You understand what's happening, but still, you fail to express it in words. When it comes to two queens, honeybees just know, and maybe we can relate to that better than we realize. I learned this lesson again in my own life not that long ago.

When I was in the early days of getting my business started, I wanted to grow as fast as possible. You know the feeling when you are starting fresh, and you have all the opportunities at your hand. You push yourself to become successful without realizing that working smart and consistently outweighs working hard and without direction, but you do that anyway. I've already described in an earlier chapter my ill-fated Santa photos debacle—a move meant to grow us exponentially overnight, but that just ended up costing us time and money.

Another idea I had was to grow my business quickly through a merger. I looked for a long time for a CEO of another company very similar to my own with whom I could combine forces. I held countless meetings and shook a lot of hands in search of my kindred spirit, but almost every time, I either walked away with the wrong feeling, or they did because I never heard from them again. The supposed merger was another attempt in making things turn in my favor without putting much thought into it. I knew that a merger could be beneficial for the company and me, but the how and when questions in this equation were always the missing elements.

Finally, I met someone I thought was the right collaborator. He was also looking to expand quickly, and we had the same general dreams and philosophy for our businesses. We set our sights on forming one company, which would be one of the largest photography companies in North America. We worked together for months to establish what the company would look like, how we would launch it, and what our roles would be. Basically, we stretched out a possible future, thinking where the company could go if we plan certain roles and moves accordingly.

We were nearing the end of the process and engaged in a two-day focus meeting where we were hashing out some of the details when I started to get this feeling. I was sitting in the boardroom with this other CEO going over the specifics of the deal and the future of our company, and something just felt off. Nothing significant had changed, no bombshells had been dropped or eleventh-hour revelations made—it was more of a gnawing, growing suspicion that was slowly enveloping me. You might even call it a "vibe."

I found myself thinking back to that story I'd been telling for so long, the one about the second queen bee hatching and about learning the hard way what a swarm looks like, about understanding when it's time to split the hive. I kept thinking about that question: "Without the beekeeper doing it for her, how does the queen know when to leave the hive?"

All that time, I'd been answering, "She just knows. She gets a 'vibe.'" There I was, sitting in my own boardroom, thinking, "I don't know if this opportunity is right." My role here resembled that of a queen, and I needed a beekeeper who could navigate me or place me in a position where I'd "just know" when to make the transition.

At first, I tried to ignore the feeling. I tried to quiet it down and distract myself. Then I tried to reason with it. I questioned whether I was getting cold feet about growing so quickly and perhaps experiencing discomfort because of the complexities that would be involved, but I knew in my heart it wasn't that. I wasn't nervous because of growth or change or upcoming challenges. Something just didn't feel right.

I decided to sleep on it, and when I got up, I decided to think about it over breakfast. And then lunch. And then dinner. And then sleep on it again. I honestly hoped the feeling would diminish because I'd looked for so long and so hard for the right partner and to hammer out the right deal. I was on the verge of being the co-CEO of the largest photography company in North America. It seemed ludicrous to throw it all away on a "feeling." The new co-CEO title of the largest photography company in North America seemed daunting in my thoughts. At times, my thoughts would tell me to drop it all, while at other times, they'd point me in the direction of prosperity by hinting that this is it.

When I woke up the morning after that and the feeling was still there, I knew I couldn't ignore it any longer. I thought of my honeybees, of how when there are two queens, they know it's time to go. My own instincts had kicked in, and they were telling me that, despite the potential pain, it was time for me to go too.

This is the story I have been telling you since the beginning. The two queens single hive story or two alpha lions in a single jungle theory never struck me so clearly before this moment. I paralleled the hive with the company and the queens with myself and my partner, and instantly I got the bigger picture. For once, while deciding the biggest decision of my life, I hyper-focused by charting a comparison of my human life with a honeybee. The answer was immediately in front of me, and it was devoid of any doubts whatsoever. After all, it had to make sense. Because like a honeybee who works for the sustenance of a hive, we humans do the same for corporations.

I wrote to my mentor, Graham McFarland, about my concerns. Graham has been my mentor for twenty years—he knows me and my quick-start nature, but he also knows that I have good instincts and that I shouldn't ignore what my gut tells me. "Give it twenty-four hours," he wrote.

I laughed. "I already did that," I wrote back.

After a moment, he responded: "Then I guess you know what to do."

I decided to kill the deal. I sent a message that simply said it wasn't right for me anymore and that I was out. Then I waited to be swarmed.

I knew when I made that decision; it would be a hard change. It'd be a human version of how I saw the appearance of swarm and reduction in worker bee class. I was right. I did lose half my workers, and for those of us who remained, it felt like we were wandering, looking for a new place in the woods—at least figuratively. I'd been focused on my vision of a huge, ambitious company, and I now had to recalibrate to determine what I really wanted. I had to take my team and find a new hive, so to speak. Once again, I felt like that hive queen who wanted a place for herself and her workers and who wanted to keep her worker bees employed in doing the tasks they are supposed to do. I felt the same. I pressed the reset button by parting ways, which essentially meant find a new place, new framework, and new ways to do the same as what we were doing before the split.

In the end, with time to reflect on what went wrong, I realized I had that vibe because there were fundamental differences in our philosophies as CEOs that would've been impossible to overcome.

What I've learned, both from my honeybees and my own personal experience is simply this: two CEOs is never a good idea. Two minds leading a company is similar to two queens giving different instructions to their workers. The wave-length of communication, or in human terms, the medium of message deliverance that came to workers was from the higher authority. However, even then, there was still confusion in interpretation. There's just no way to avoid confusion, distraction, and waste. Two CEOs is a prime example of a divided focus. You can't focus on one philosophy, one direction, or one goal when you have two people in charge. Each CEO has a particular way of looking at the company's framework and planning the roadmap accordingly. Then there comes a difference of opinion and execution in a certain style which may conflict with the ideologies of the other one. This is quite similar to why we don't have two presidents of the United States because although we have two major political parties, only one can be in charge at a time. Think about how difficult it could get if we, or any other country for that matter, had two presidents.

However, the real problem with co-CEOs will come while they are carrying out their duties as both of them will have to look at the matters from a shared perspective and will have to act in unison. Similarly, there's a reason you don't hear about two CEOs at Microsoft, Facebook, or Uber.

We talked in the last chapter about the importance of your company's culture and how that standard and tone for everybody at the company is set from the top-down, starting with the CEO. When you have two CEOs, it's virtually impossible to establish a consistent culture. Every queen bee multiplies; similarly, CEOs have their own protégés and devotees. With two CEOs, you'll end up with one group of people subscribing to one style of communication and another group subscribing to something different.

The biggest problem in working with two CEOs is that you do not precisely know "who is the boss;" you are always confused about where the orders are coming from. Also, a lot of companies with co-CEOs are found to suffer from high potential ego issues. Whenever they disagree with each other, it creates a conflict in the company, which causes a great deal of disturbance among employees. Therefore, the idea of multiple CEOs or founders in the corporate world is a total mess.

Within these years, I have learned that employees need a specific sense of direction to work peacefully. Just like a beehive, your company also has some particular operations that need to be carried out on an everyday basis. Now, what would happen if a "second queen bee" comes from nowhere and starts intervening in the daily tasks of honeybees? It would be a mess, right? Well, the same happens in real life too. Two CEOs means "two minds;" no matter how much the similarity, your opinions cannot match with the other person every time. Sometimes you have to disagree, and this is where things go sore, especially in the corporate world. Both CEOs want to benefit the company but have different views. It could lead to a total failure at times.

Now, as with most rules, there are occasional exceptions. Every once in a while, you'll come across two CEOs of a successful endeavor who seem to have worked everything out with a solid system in place. In these situations, they almost always have one thing in common: they're married to each other (or they're life partners). Other than that, this arrangement is rarely found in businesses. I have seen very few companies that had two CEOs at a time and were running peacefully. Sometimes, such companies can become a huge success too, but the conflict remains somewhat there.

Many small businesses in America replicate this dynamic, with married couples working together as restaurateurs, accountants, medical practitioners, or in whatever type of small business they've started. These are the exceptions to the "one queen bee" rule, and there are a few reasons they're able to pull it off. Needless to say, those CEOs must have a sure-fire formula of respecting each other's decisions.

Finally, if they're lucky, most married couples are also in love, which means they might prioritize the other person's happiness, making them more likely to seek agreement when issues arise.

You may have heard of another photojournalist and beekeeper who turned his hobby into a lucrative business: Burt Shavitz, the late founder of Burt's Bees, one of the most popular brands of all-natural cosmetics, skincare, and hygiene products available on the market.

After serving in the Army, Burt Shavitz worked as a photographer in the 1960s, photographing anti-war rallies and

John F. Kennedy for publications for the *New York Times* and *Time Life*. It was a career he ditched for a simpler life peddling honey by the side of the road.

Shavitz had stumbled on a swam of honeybees in the 1970s that had congregated on a fencepost. With the help of a beekeeper friend, he transported the honeybees to a hive. It was the first of 26 beehives for Burt, who used an inheritance to purchase some land in Maine. He started selling honey jars on the side of the road. That's where he met Roxanne Quimby, a graphic designer and marketer who became his romantic and business partner and helped launch the company into stardom.

But when their romantic relationship went south, the whole endeavor turned rather vicious, with lawsuits and backstabbing business deals muddying what was once a great partnership. In the end, Burt lost millions of dollars—but even more than that, it cost him his vision of the company and culture he'd wanted. Burt's bees founder Burt Shavitz died on July 5, 2015 at age 80.

Here are some things to think about when confronting this potential scenario:

Be prepared for the unexpected. Sometimes you can anticipate and avoid conflict by getting ahead of potential problems. In your mind, think about all the worst scenarios that can take place with that specific person. Think about the final outcome of your decision. Would you be able to deal with any future conflicts or disputes?

You need to take a look at your patience levels once again

before you make this major decision. Before you get completely associated with them, ask yourself whether or not you can take criticism. Or, how much value do you hold for other people's choices and opinions? Because one thing is for sure, multiple CEOs means numerous mindsets; you cannot expect the new CEO to agree with your decisions every time. There are going to be times when he/she would force you to take a particular decision or sign a specific contract but you would not be comfortable with it. So, think hard before you finally take any step for yourself and your company.

Call in a business coach or consultants with experience if you need them. Needless to say, an experienced professional always knows better than every entrepreneur and CEO. If you are confused about your decision, simply talk to a coach or some experienced consultant. Tell them about your phobias, fears, and concerns attached to your decisions. I am sure they would be able to guide you much better. And you will definitely find a way out.

If you can avoid a "swarm" by making changes in an orderly, well-thought-out process, you'll increase your chances of success.

At a certain point, you have to let nature take its course. Listen to your instincts. Sometimes a "vibe" is more than just a vibe—it's a premonition of future problems. Hear closely what your gut feeling indicates. It can really hint about the right or wrong decisions that you are about to take. And also the risks attached to your decision of indulging multiple CEOs in your business.

Think about things for twenty-four hours before acting rashly (The 24-Hour Rule). Decisions taken in any sort of anger, extreme happiness, or depression are never healthy. You need to give yourself some time to think about the consequences of your action. Consider all the pros and cons of your decisions.

You can share a philosophy and ambition with another person, but it doesn't mean your company cultures will be in sync—and contrasting company cultures can lead to chaos in the office.

Married couples or life partners can sometimes beat the odds and become successful business partners, but it's a risk. Think long and hard before you put all your eggs in one basket.

I have realized that every person has his/her unique purpose of existence, just like the honeybees. Your role cannot be carried out by someone else. No matter what position you hold in your company, you believe in the collective objective of staying true and committed to your workplace. Just like the beehive, all the employees work hard to achieve the same goal. From the queen bee to all the worker bees, everyone in the hive aims to get more and more nectar from the plants to meet their targets.

There's a lot to learn from the honeybees and their systematic work, especially for the entrepreneurs and new CEOs. We need to apply the same approach as honeybees to our lives. This can benefit us not only in our professional but also personal lives. For example, whenever a honeybee is itchy, another bee immediately jumps on her back and comforts her. As Jacqueline Freeman, author of *Song of Increase*, puts in, *"A worker bee in need of grooming will dance to signal her need for assistance until a fellow worker comes to her aid."* This shows the connection between honeybees and their incredible harmony and will to help each other. I think we all need to implement the same policy in our lives too. We need to offer all our support and help to the co-workers who are in need, not only because they work in the same company, but also because we are all humans. We need to uplift each other in order to prosper in the long run.

Also, another interesting fact is that honeybees have their specific way of dancing to hint the other honeybees about the best plants around! They kind of do that little "waggle dance" to attract the attention of the other honeybees. It is the signal to indicate that the best nectar is found here! Isn't that amazing? I remember that I was so amazed when I read this. I think we all need to instill the same positivity in our lives too. We need to offer a helping hand to each and every person who is in need. And also tell them about the best sources around that can benefit them. Just like honeybees, you and I can also work together to ensure that our community thrives and prospers with our immense dedication and support towards work.

I believe that nothing is more amazing about humans than our immense innovative abilities and willpower. We have been designed to achieve whatever we want through our extraordinary dedication and skills. When we have the confidence and courage to be consistent, no obstacle seems insurmountable. Humans can be just as compassionate towards society as honeybees, but only if they become willing to lend a helping hand to others. You need to get into that right mind frame to achieve the same organization, planning, and expertise in your work that a honeybee has. You can easily implement this "honeybee mindset" in your life if you focus on being more attentive, communicative, and alert towards your work. Life is just as complicated as we think it is. This world can truly become a better place if we absorb these lessons from honeybees as individuals. We can surely foster these learnings in others and spread positivity everywhere we go. With our collective efforts, I am sure we will soon achieve that dynamic and peaceful community that has always been a dream.

**Buzzing Points**

Here are some things to think about when confronting this question:

• Be prepared for the unexpected. Sometimes you can anticipate and avoid conflict by getting ahead of potential problems. In your mind, think about all the worst scenarios that can take place with that specific person. Think about the final outcome of your decision. Would you be able to deal with any future conflicts or disputes?

• You need to take a look at your patience levels once again before you make this major decision. Before you get completely associated with them, ask yourself whether or not you can take criticism. Or, how much value do you hold for other people's choices and opinions? Because one thing is for sure, multiple CEOs mean numerous mindsets; you cannot expect the new CEO to agree with your decisions every time.

• Call in a business coach or consultants with experience if you need them. An experienced professional always knows better than every entrepreneur and CEO. If you are confused about your decision, talk to a coach or some experienced consultant. Tell them about your phobias, fears, and concerns attached to your choices. I am sure they would be able to guide you much better. And you will find a way out.

• If you can avoid a "swarm" by making changes in an orderly, well-thought-out process, you'll increase your chances of success.

• At a certain point, you have to let nature take its course. Listen to your instincts. Sometimes a "vibe" is more than just a vibe—it's a premonition of future problems. Hear closely to what your gut feeling indicates. It can hint at you about the right or wrong decisions that you are about to take and also the risks attached to your decision of indulging multiple CEOs in your business.

# Why Do Some Hives Thrive and Some Hives Die?

If you pay attention to the news, you may have heard about a crisis within the honeybee community over the last few years. The Colony Collapse Disorder, or CCD for short. It is a sudden, alarming uptick in the colony collapse of beehives that has had a devastating effect on our ecosystem. Honeybees are essential to that ecosystem. It's not just that they provide honey that we love. They are also a source of beeswax, which is used in many products, not to mention honeybees play a significant role in our society in numerous other aspects. They are a source of pollination. Every time a honeybee visits a flower, some of the pollen from the plant latches onto the honeybee. The honeybee then visits numerous flowers, and every visit spreads pollens everywhere. Another aspect is vegetation. Due to cross-pollination, plants thrive and grow wherever the honeybee travels. This helps spread vegetation all over the planet and helps the flora flourish.

Honeybees are fundamentally ingrained in our society as an integral part of our livelihood. It is said that one out of every three meals consumed by people is possible because of honeybees. If honeybees were to die out, thousands of plants would follow suit, and the consequence of that is millions of humans starving to death. Although we aren't directly consuming the honeybees, their existence is imperative for humans to thrive. Foods like apples, pumpkins, onions, coffee, and many plants that are fed to livestock would no longer be available. No matter how small these creatures of nature look, they have considerable responsibilities interwoven into their routine.

So, why are honeybees dying? The answer to that questions depends on whom you ask. There are many hypotheses on what leads to colony collapse, but there's probably not just a single cause. It is an amalgamation of multiple reasons. Whether it's cell phone towers interfering with honeybee communications, pesticides killing foragers in the fields, or disease ravaging the colonies from the inside out, there are likely a few different explanations for why some hives are dying.

## The Colony Collapse Disorder

It is undeniable that honeybees are quite instrumental in helping humans thrive on earth, so it makes sense that people should ensure that honeybees thrive as well and don't go extinct. For that very purpose, it is a good idea to understand how the honeybees are dying and how we can save them.

The first cause for concern is the use of pesticides. To be more specific, the use of neonicotinoids. Neonicotinoid is a chemical compound that is similar to nicotine. It was first approved for use as a pesticide in the 1990s. At the time, chemicals like DDT (Dichlorodiphenyltrichloroethane) were quite prevalent in society as a popular insecticide. However, it was later revealed that DDT has numerous environmental health risks both to wildlife and humans, so its use for pesticides was discontinued. From then on, neonicotinoids rose to popularity.

Neonicotinoids can be used in various crops like rice, cereal grains, nuts, grapes, apples, oranges, peaches, cherries, berries, potatoes, tomatoes, and leafy greens, among many more. If you think about it, so much of our diet consists of these crops. The chemical compound is sprayed onto plants and spreads to water. When honeybees come in contact with either of those, they get infected with the toxin. Adding to this, the toxin spreads to other honeybees as well because they inevitably return to the hive.

When honeybees come into contact with heavy doses of the toxin, they can experience paralysis, convulsions, and even death. Another way the honeybees are harmed is that the neonicotinoids intoxicate the honeybee's senses (similar to nicotine). This, in turn, leads to the honeybees losing their way in the wild and being unable to return to the hive. Although neonicotinoids are banned in many countries, they are still somewhat in use in Europe, which is a cause for concern.

Another reason for CCD is diversification. The term that's commonly used for this is Modern Monoculture Agriculture. To commercialize and make the most out of crops, modern farmers plant the same race of crops in their fields. This makes it easier for them to harvest the crops as well as provide them nutrition. However, a consequence of this tactic is the monotonous routine honeybees are subjected to.

Think of it this way. If you're given the same food twice a day, every day, sooner or later, you're going to get tired of it. It's not just the idea of boredom. Honeybees need a diverse and rich diet of food to survive. With Monoculture Agriculture surrounding the honeybees, they need to go out of their way and travel extra distance to have a proper diet. Their laborious routine is further intensified as a result. This causes the honeybees to wander off of the fields into villages and other areas that are hazardous to their health and tedious to traverse. The honeybees then either come back feeling tired or don't come back at all.

This creates another problem that is a major reason for CCD. When honeybees come back tired, weak, or don't get enough food, their immune system becomes vulnerable. Honeybees have many enemies in nature, and they take complete advantage of the weakened state of honeybees. These enemies range from viruses, parasites, and all kinds of bacteria.

A commonly found bacteria is the Acarapis Woodi. It is a dangerous bacteria that infiltrates the breathing system of the honeybees. Inside their body, it lays eggs in their trachea, which makes it harder for the honeybees to breathe. Feeding on the bodily fluids of the honeybees, they act as a parasite, weakening their prey until they suffocate.

One of the greatest parasitic threats to honeybees is the Varroa Destructor. This dangerous parasite only reproduces in honeybee hives, making them a natural nemesis for the honeybees. This parasite infiltrates the beehives and lays its eggs on the honeybee larva before it pupates. This is strategically done before the honeybees cover the cell with a wax capping. Once the cell is closed off with wax, the eggs hatch and attack the developing honeybee. The wax sealing still protects them, so the parasites are actually protected from all of their threats.

Although the honeybee isn't killed at this stage, it is definitely weakened after which the newly developed honeybee chews through the wax capping. When this is done, the parasite spreads to other cells, reproducing and attacking other unprotected honeybee larvae. Within a span of a few months, the entire honeybee hive collapses as the parasite weakens all of its hosts. Not to mention, they suck body fluids from adult honeybees and infect them with numerous deadly viruses that can cause honeybees to grow with birth defects. These viruses cause honeybees to grow with unusually small wings, which prevent them from flying and renders them useless.

On paper, all of these are dangerous reasons for honeybees to disappear, yet they are not enough on their own to cause CCD. Modern urbanization like cell phone towers and crowded cities harm the honeybee's chances of survival as well. It's hard to pinpoint one cause for the death of honeybees, as all of the above serves as an amalgamation of honeybee deaths.

So how do we go about fixing this mess? Beekeepers may be able to prevent problems in their own backyards if they pay attention to their honeybees and hives. If not, who else will protect this species? If the failure is allowed to continue and (without beekeepers), honeybees will be wiped from the face of the earth. For this very reason, I am in constant contact with my hives. I keep my eyes on the honeybees' productivity. I use their performance as a barometer for their health. At the same time, I know what's going on around us in the world outside of my backyard. I know where there might be spraying, and I know which way the wind is blowing. I also know the proximity of cell towers, and I keep an eye on the diseases that are out there and how they might be spreading. All in all, when I am inside my backyard, I tend to care for the honeybees and the hives as best as I can in a direct manner. However, whenever I am outside, my consciousness continuously looks for possible hazards that can harm the honeybees. One has to go through such lengths to make sure that their investment and honeybees, in general, are safe, especially after the recent incident involving endangerment to the bee-kind.

When it comes to your business, it's a similar situation. There are factors in the wider environment that are beyond your control, and there are factors in your immediate surroundings for which you can prepare. When you own something, you have to give it 100%. It then genuinely does not matter if things are not in your control. You have to consistently try to outdo yourself in bringing betterment for your business because that is how your company flourishes. Similarly, if changes occur that impact your beekeeping, it's up to you to examine which factors affected you the most. You have to narrow down which ones you can control or which ones you can't see coming. Whatever the case be, it is you who gets to be vigilant. Without your active involvement, who do you think will look after your business (or beekeeping in my case)? In this way, the success of your business often comes down to storytelling.

## The power of storytelling

There's a confluence of factors that affect the success or failure of a company, just as they do with beehives. On paper, we may hypothesize why a colony collapses, but there's only so much current science to back up those ideas. Based on what we know or whatever the science discovered, we try our level best to connect the dots and find a logical explanation. It is up to us to fill in the gaps. However, there is no guarantee that the final conclusion we do reach in the end accurately backs up our hypothesis.

So, what can we do in such scenarios? In the end, we have to fill in the gaps with a story—a narrative that connects one fact to another—to make sense of it all. The literal meaning of a story can be a chain of events that happen that cause characters to progress and develop. In our case, we can adopt this definition in a slightly different manner. For us, the chain of events is the different reasons that harm the honeybees, while the progression of the characters is essentially the progression of our honeybees. From a business perspective, it is imperative to understand what events took place and how the characters (employees and leaders) dealt with them. We may know in certain cases exactly what happened to cause the success or failure of a company, but there's no formula that definitively spells out which businesses will live and which will die. Life is uncertain, to say the least. All of the developments are left for the happening. Until something has not unfolded, there is no saying in which path will it go.

**" We may know in certain cases exactly what happened to cause the success or failure of a company, but there's no formula that definitively spells outwhich businesses will live and which will die. "**

For example, it may seem to an outsider that a ski resort went out of business because no snow fell on the mountain that year. Yes, that certainly wouldn't have helped, but what that version of the story doesn't account for is what preparation may have been done in anticipation of this eventuality. Was the CEO consulting experts early on? Did he look at technological solutions? Did he reallocate money to adjust for possible lost revenue? Or did he just cross his fingers and hope for the best, ignoring the warnings and proceeding with business as usual? This is one of the prime examples where you miss the point of connecting the right story with the accurate set of events that happened. This is why many fail to comprehend what exactly happened or how did the abysmal fate of a company come.Until you understand why you failed, you cannot succeed, for it is the lesson learned in failure that leads to success.

As I write this book, a pandemic has seized the world. COVID-19 has shaken everything to its core, and America is suffering just as the rest of the world. Americans are in lockdown. Those of us who are lucky are working from home, while others are risking their lives on the frontlines as healthcare providers or essential workers. Some of us have lost our jobs, or worse, died from the deadly virus itself. We're only weeks into what is sure to be a long-term crisis, and already, countless businesses are on their last legs. This health disaster is ravaging the American economy in ways not seen since the Great Depression. Just as some beehives collapse because of viruses, many businesses are facing the same fate for the same reason. A virus doesn't care about your personal ambition, hard work, or innovation. It's an indiscriminate killer, and there will be many casualties, human, and otherwise. It serves the purpose for which it is made of—to invade the host, takeover its system, and leave it lifeless like a dead shell.

The story we'll hear in the future is that COVID-19 was a not-so-silent killer within many industries. In some cases, this will be proven to be true, but if we look back carefully, beyond the storytelling, the truth may not be so simple. As of Christmas 2019, the forecast for many major retailers was already bleak. Headlines mentioned major retailers going bankrupt long before the coronavirus slammed the United States in early 2020. Yet when this moment in history is examined, it will be "story time" for a lot of these companies. The timeline will be compressed, and giants that went under for reasons other than COVID-19 will be lumped together with those that were legitimately affected by the virus. It is all about viewing the overall picture and portraying the set pieces as you see them, not how they happened. It is because the history that we learn is often told from a narrator's perspective. We are seldom witnesses to the events happening, so we have to rely on the storyteller to tell a coherent and truthful story. Ever heard the phrase, "If you tell a lie big enough and keep repeating it, people will eventually come to believe it?" That is the exact premise behind crafting a story. It is an excuse which, if executed in an ideal manner, can operate as "the big lie." For example, years after a war, a pandemic, or a great recession, people will hardly focus or pinpoint at the plausible cause. However, they will hear stories about the repercussions, not the reasons which expedited the birth of these problems in the first place.

Why does this matter? That is because the story you tell yourself and others about the trajectory of your business is important. It will affect your future behavior, the decisions you make, and the way you're perceived by others. It will create an overall image that not only will be a compass for many aspiring businessmen but it also will dictate the future prospects of your business. Based on the story you tell about your company, you will start to believe in what you actually tell as a story that to what actually happened. You will begin to believe in whatever you say instead of whatever you did.

When people ask me about a deal that went bad, I always start my answer with, "This is *my* story about what happened. Someone else might have a different version, but from my perspective, this is what went down." I do this to establish a baseline that whatever I am about to say does not necessarily represent how it happened. What I speak is my version of the truth based on how I observed things from my perspective and how I was opinionated by it. It is the view of something based on how I approached it, saw it, and to the best of my knowledge, understood it.

Furthermore, I do this because, as much as I might try, my understanding is always going to be limited by my own perspective. There may be things I don't know or versions of the story I don't agree with. I have to acknowledge that, as hard as I've worked to understand the full picture, it's still just a *story* that I'm telling to make sense of my experience. You have a right to your version of the story when it comes to the success or failure of your business, as do other company owners when it comes to theirs. However, *what* story you choose to tell can make a huge difference for your company's future. It is morally correct for one to tell a story that accurately reflects the truth.

Think about it like this: the story you tell will become a looking glass through which you or others will start to see your company. If you hide the reasons for your failure, not only will you see this as an excuse, but others as well will start thinking of it as a reckless or irresponsible way to deal with the situation.

## Fact vs. fiction

We've all known people who have an excuse for everything:

"I would've been here on time, but a cop with nothing better to do pulled me over for speeding."

"I was going to have that report ready, but my computer crashed."

"Look, I would get along with my coworkers fine if they would just listen to what I say."

These are expert storytellers, but not in a good way. The truth of a situation *is* often relative and sometimes not totally knowable. However, if you find yourself constantly in a bind but don't feel you're ever at fault, chances are you aren't seeing the whole picture. It's essential to recognize your own role in these situations, or you'll be doomed to repeat them.

Storytelling can work for you or against you. There are the fairytales you create just to make yourself feel better, and then there are the fact-based stories, grounded in as much information as possible, that allow you to learn from a situation. Which story you tell is up to you.

Over many years of having those three o'clock coffees with others, I have been treated to countless stories of great business acumen and success. However, the truth is, I learn just as much, if not more, from the stories of epic failures. Many of the people that I met with had been involved in multiple businesses. By the time we met, they were sometimes well into a fifth or sixth attempt. I saw it all the time: a person would have a great idea, start a business, and then get to a certain level and close it. The businesses were all different kinds of endeavors, but they all had one thing in common—there was always a story behind why it all went wrong. Spoiler alert: it was rarely the CEO's fault.

The stories I heard always involved external factors, such as an economic downturn, unforeseen technological changes, or a poor location for a brick-and-mortar store. Why? That is because they are simple yet loosely related to the reality. It is why many conceive this idea of blaming every external factor they could possibly think of. External factors, after all, are not in your control. It's a great scapegoat for one to blame their problems on. Some good storytellers make excuses and conceive ideas to back it up out of thin air. Within a matter of minutes, they have a sage tale of failure to tell—not necessarily based on how it happened, though. Sometimes the external factor involved other people, like an unsupportive board, a lack of reliable employees, or a competitor with an unfair advantage. At one meeting, I spoke to someone who'd started six kinds of businesses that had all failed. Surprisingly, he was about to open a seventh. I finally asked, "What makes you think the seventh business is going to be any different from the last six?"

He didn't have a good answer because he was truly convinced that what he was doing was right and everything around him was wrong. The issue was that his personal storytelling was getting in the way of his success. He didn't want to face the cold, hard facts about what went wrong, and so he'd crafted a narrative that made him feel better. I knew as long as he continued to do that, his seventh business was going to go the same way as his first six. This is what I have been emphasizing so excessively. The failed attempts you get and the stories you make around it actually shape your perspective of how you progress. In the above-mentioned case, the businessman I spoke with had made up his mind that he needed to keep trying. He believed that success was within reach, and he just needed to try once more. This ideology did push him to try for better or for worse. However, his story was devoid of all the facts that contributed to making his business ventures a failure. Had he been a good storyteller, the kind who includes all the details despite how they see the overall picture, he could have pulled off to become a better businessman with his 2nd or 3rd attempt. His failure is credited to his narration of how he failed, pushing him to do the same thing again, just hoping for a better outcome.

I am not emphasizing the idea that failing is a bad omen in the business. Actually, failure is a part of business, and you have to expect it on some level. Not only should you expect it, but you should learn as much as you can from it when it does arise. However, when you're examining what went wrong, especially if it has gone wrong multiple times, you must consider the story that you're telling isn't altogether accurate. You have to go back, reread those chapters, look at the ending you've given them, and consider making some radical changes, the kind of ones that mirror closely with the actual data.

At the same time, storytelling can be a powerful tool for positivity in your entrepreneur's arsenal. Throughout my career, I've taken this to the extreme by making my storytelling literal: I've written books. It gives me great satisfaction, personally and professionally, to use my storytelling skills to help other people who are looking to start or expand their businesses. You don't always need to be an author to benefit from the right kind of storytelling. All you need to do is reflect what was true when you are trying to tell a story about your business, a memorable success, or an abysmal failure. It helps you set a trajectory enabling you to advance on the path you think is right.

Seeing the big picture and understanding where things went off the rails can prove beneficial to you in the future. You can then understand what you did wrong and what you could've done right. It also helps if you understand the narrative of a successful business and how that business will function when things change. As I write this, the COVID-19 outbreak is still in its earliest stages, but it's already clear that the pandemic will likely change much of the world as we know it. The pandemic has frozen everything to a standstill, and it is hard to imagine life the way it was years ago.

My business, Photos in a Minute, is all about high-volume

photography—providing quick, quality photos for hundreds (sometimes thousands) of people at a time during huge events. As "social distancing" becomes the new normal, my company's reality will also have to change. The story of my company centers on providing customer service, helping people create and preserve memories, and offering an excellent product in a timely manner. I don't know yet exactly how we'll adapt to this new normal, but understanding our story will certainly help me to figure it out. It will allow me to chart a pattern in which the new world order is shaping towards a viable manner of business. Knowing what I am supposed to expect will allow me to see a foreseeable future, at least a prospective version of it, where I will have a chance of tackling my business by adapting to the radical changes post-COVID world demands. If not, without the prior knowledge of what will become the new norm, I will be advancing into an unknown territory. Not only will it be devastating for my future business career, but it can also become a mistake of a lifetime. Pandemics like COVID-19 only happen once per century, or so we are taught by history. The last century had the Spanish flu, and this one has COVID-19. In any case, these events demand far-reaching measures, and I, too, in such an instance, need to present the accurate image of my business to myself first and to the others later.

My personal story as a business person and entrepreneur will also help me adjust to the changing times. Successful CEOs and companies have to learn to pivot during challenging times. You're not a successful business person if you don't know how to adapt and learn on the fly. Over the years, I've acquired so much knowledge and experience that I've developed a desire to diversify, expanding my brand to be about more than photography as social norms change due to the current public-health situation.

I also believe people with ADHD, like myself, have an extreme ability to hyper-focus on the "One Thing" during stressful times. People with ADHD will wait until the very last minute, then hyper-focus on that test, project, or work proposal just before the deadline is due. Another word for it is procrastination which is a commonly found problem. Now add a pandemic to the equation, and people like myself will go into what I call "Hyper Bee Focused" mode.

During the COVID-19 pandemic in 2020, I was speaking to my good friend and a person I look up to, Dr. Ned Hallowell. Ned is the world's leading expert on ADHD and Attention Deficit Disorders and has written multiple bestsellers on the subject, including one of my favorites, *Driven to Distraction*. Ned agreed with my beliefs during times of crisis.

I have the ability to focus forward into the future, whether we are in the midst of a crisis or not, because of my positive mindset. I keep a Focus Forward worksheet in my journal, and when I look back on it, I often find that I accomplish almost 80% of my goals sooner than I planned. This practice of taking a peek into the foreseeable future did not always have an 80% success ratio. My habit of doing it frequently, over the course of the past 20 years, has perfected it. I believe, at some point or other, a businessman had to keep a Focus Forward worksheet. It essentially involves looking at the patterns from the past and charting a way forward—the accuracy of it comes from how closely you picture yourself. It could also be because I like to hyper-focus on things, and the development of this concept came naturally to me as a result of ADHD. In any case, the Focus Forward routine helps me strike the perfect balance in diving into what is necessary and getting out of it whenever it does more harm than good. That is because ADHD does not always warrant a productive hyper-focus. You can very well be using this ability to analyze.

I can see myself shifting more focus to my coaching business, using my experiences to help people emerge from this crisis, reboot, and rebuild bigger and better than before. I'll be able to do this not only because my personal story is strong but also because I found my "One Thing," which is doing what you love and helping other people while doing it.

What I'm describing when I talk about using your story in this way is really about developing a mindset.

## Developing the right mindset

From an early age, I was always intrigued by what it meant to run my own business. I've never had a "regular" job with a supervisor or a boss to learn from, so how could I form a mindset, company culture, or business philosophy in which I had confidence? One benefit to being in the photography business was having access to many very successful business people and leaders—for example, working in the White House, I was able to observe a president, Barack Obama, who was truly at the top of his field.

I knew early on that if I surrounded myself with successful people, I would start to think like them. This sounds simple, but it can actually be quite challenging. For one thing, you might have to invest in high-end coaching programs or training seminars to gain access to these types of leaders. Also, surrounding yourself with highly successful people can be intimidating. You get the feeling of sinking in when considering their accomplishments sometimes. It necessarily does not serve in drowning your motives and objectives to excel in something you believe. What I believe is, intimidating or not, surrounding yourself with people who have experience and sophistication in a particular field always teaches you something that could be learned years away from that point. That is because it is the exposure that counts. You get to know about them first hand. It also feels overwhelming to know how much such a person has achieved in a little time.

I remember attending my first professional development workshop, surrounded by people I thought of as rock stars—multimillionaire CEOs of wildly successful companies. I was a photographer and doing quite well, with multiple business locations nationwide. However, I was still quite nervous when it came time for me to introduce myself and, in particular, the successful photography pop-up shops of Santa photos I'd built. One fellow was particularly unimpressed, or perhaps he just had an ungenerous sense of humor: as I introduced myself and described my business, he chuckled and said, "Santa, huh? Maybe you can go after the Easter Bunny next."

Everybody laughed, and for a moment, my heart was in my

throat. But as I stood there in the front row (I always grab the first seat in the front row at workshops), I simply smiled and said, "Actually, that's how I got started, taking pictures for the Easter Egg Roll in the Obama White House. It was President Obama who gave me the positive reinforcement to grow my company nationwide and do more, which pushed me harder to launch the Santa Claus photos experience pop-up shops."

You could hear a pin drop. Suddenly, I had transformed from small potatoes to a major player. Part of that was because I'd associated myself with one of the most successful people in the world. But upon reflection, I think it was more than that for me. Maybe, on some level, when I said "Barrack Obama," they developed that I am not just a regular photographer who covers Santa related photoshoots. They began to take me seriously the moment I associated myself with someone, who according to them, is a notable or successful person in his line of work. However, it may very well be a reason for them. I personally believe that President Obama's encouragement to be more for me was the one I required to push myself for the next big thing. I had it in me, and by simply surrounding myself with a top-tier personality, I did a service to myself in developing my future self. When I introduced myself, I was reflecting on the intimidation I felt. My voice wasn't confident. My body language showed uncertainty. Yet when I was teased, I found that inner strength and stood up a little straighter. I began reflecting on the self-assuredness I was seeing in the other people around the room; I started to embody the idea that I belonged there. "No, I have nothing to be ashamed of," my posture and tone said in response to the jab. "I'm not out of my depth. I have something to offer here."

That was truly a defining moment for me. In that split second, I realized that what you do is far less important than how much you believe in your own story. From that moment on, I was able to approach people with confidence. I knew what I was building, how many people it reached, and what my goals were. My mindset allowed me to walk into any room and hold my own, and it allowed me to call other CEOs out of the blue and invite them out for coffee.

## Allowing your story to change as you grow

It might sound ironic, but one of the most valuable traits for developing a strong, successful mindset is *open-mindedness*. An ability to consider all possibilities and not fixate on a predetermined plan allows you to roll with the punches, as well as to observe other people's practices and novel ideas. When you see someone doing something totally brilliant, rather than give in to envy or resentment, consider how you might adopt a similar practice. I'm *happy* when I see someone else's company thriving because I don't believe it has to be a zero-sum game the way some people try to make it. If you keep your business original and vibrant, you'll find your clients. Seeing someone else's success drives me to find my own version, the angle that makes what *I'm* doing special in my particular market.

You also have to be able to transition for personal reasons. A global pandemic can throw a wrench in your plans—or it can cause a change of heart on what you'd like to do going forward. Something new and exciting might reveal itself to you, or your passions may take you in a different direction. You need to be true to yourself and learn to adapt with the times. You can't afford to stay in denial based on what other around say or do.

When I was a freelance photographer, jet-setting around the world taking photos, I never dreamed I'd develop the ambition to write multiple books or open a private, elite coaching company. When I was diagnosed and treated for my ADHD, I had no idea it would lead me on the path to becoming a focus expert and expanding my brand beyond anything I ever thought possible. However, as the years progressed and the opportunities presented themselves, I stayed open to those possibilities. My interests changed—and so did my personal story and the story of my business.

That doesn't mean the fundamentals of my story have changed. As a photographer, I've always been able to focus on what I call my "vivid vision©," something I learned more of from Cameron Herold, whom I met at Joe Polish's *Genius Network* workshop. This is something that has served me well as my brand and story have expanded. Now I help other people focus on their own visions, empowering each of them to Focus Forward, to craft the perfect pitch or design the ideal roadmap to take the next successful steps in business and in life.

One thing I've discovered as I've allowed my story to evolve is that something you consider to be an obstacle may end up being a great asset. When I was first diagnosed with ADHD, the first question I asked my psychiatrist, Dr. William Barnard, was, "Do I have to tell anybody?"

"No, of course not," he answered. "But I hope you do decide to share your story eventually because you have a great story to share."

In that moment, I thought, "That's never going to happen." However, within twenty-four hours, a light bulb went off, and I've been finding ways to tell my story ever since. The thing that I thought would disable me in business has turned out to be one of the most important factors in my success—not only because it provides me with the ability to think big and hyper-focus, but because it gives my story an angle that makes it relatable and interesting to others.

I've told my story hundreds, probably thousands of times by now. Over the years, that story has grown to encompass a slew of tiny, relatable anecdotes with teachable moments. These are invaluable to me. Like most people, my clients don't like to be told what to do. Even when people are paying you for your professional advice, they still don't want to be lectured. It's hard to persuade anyone that way. After all, bosses are the personification of annoyance for a reason.

Storytelling is still our most useful educational tool. If you can illustrate a point through a narrative, or a relevant story that will resonate with people, you're much more likely to influence them. As many times as I've told my own story over the years, I always say: it's never really about me. It's about the listeners and the best ways to reach them. You can tell all the inspirational stories that you want, if one can not muster the spirit to put them to use, it is all in vain.

# Buzzing Points

Here are some things to keep in mind when figuring out why your company is succeeding or failing and how you can apply your storytelling skills to your benefit:

- The story you tell yourself and others about the trajectory of your business will affect your future behavior, the decisions you make, and the way you're perceived by others.

- Acknowledge your role in all mistakes and failures, or you'll never learn from them.

- You can learn just as much from stories of failure as from success stories.

- If your story always seems to end the same way, you might want to reconsider whether the story you're telling is accurate or reexamine the role you played.

- Know your own story well to help you more effectively prepare for change.

- Developing the right mindset will have a huge impact on the way you frame your story. To nurture a strong outlook that leads to success, stay open-minded. That allows you to focus on all possibilities, not simply fixate on a predetermined plan.

• Surround yourself with successful people to help you develop that mindset.

• Sometimes, something you consider to be an obstacle could end up being a great asset.

• Sharing your story is a far more effective teaching tool than simply lecturing people or telling them what to do.

# Bee Focused . . . to Bee Successful!

One of the many things I've come to appreciate about the time I've spent with my honeybees is that it forces me to take my attention off of myself. When I'm performing my beekeeper duties, I'm wholly focused on the honeybees. At that moment, I am in tune with what they're doing and what they need.

In a world full of constant networking and competition, these moments are rare gems. We're always watching ourselves through the lens of social media, trying to curate our image and control the way we're perceived by other people. When you've got the constant pressure of running a successful business, others are relying on you to make the right decisions, and the unusual circumstances brought by a global pandemic, finding the time to step outside of oneself, even for a short while, can truly be a gift.

That doesn't mean I don't think about what I'm doing when I'm with the honeybees. Quite the contrary—working with honeybees requires constant thought, attention, and energy. The idea is to channel my mind elsewhere besides work. It means I get to focus that energy outward, to not worry about how I look or what others think for just a moment. The honeybees aren't judging me; they're just being. Or "bee-ing," as the case may be. (Or as the case may "bee"—I've got a million of these and I can keep going.)

This is a valuable reminder for me and for anyone with whom I share my story: sometimes, to really accomplish something, you have to step outside of yourself, even if just for a moment or two. Whether it's honeybees, yoga, or some other hobby or discipline that occupies your thoughts for a while, it can be invaluable to think beyond yourself. We spend a lot of time navel-gazing. It's not that I have anything against deep thought, but sometimes it's useful to exercise a different muscle.

I've learned this lesson well when it comes to my own work, but it has especially served me when I'm working with others. I wanted to become an author and consultant because I believed I had stories to share. I knew that my experiences would empower me to help other people pursue their dreams, and I became passionate about sharing what I had learned on developing focus.

The more I coach, the more I find that some of my most invaluable instructors are the honeybees. Each time I open up a hive, I have to tackle the scenario with careful preparation that I have managed to channel through years of experience, and hard-fought (and won) lessons. Yet none of that means I know what I'm going to find inside the hive. All it means is that I'm well equipped to respond to whatever is waiting for me.

It's the same when it comes to coaching. My business clients expect me to be experienced and successful, but, just like the honeybees, each client ultimately has different needs, requires a different focus, and demands that I be responsive to them at the moment. You can only loosely predict the mindset and problems of the client but there are always anomalies and exceptions. Many of the lessons may be the same, but the application of those lessons will be unique, like every business or individual who comes to me for help. There's no one-size-fits-all solution that's going to solve everyone's dilemmas or provide the exact advice that everyone needs. As a coach, I'm only as effective a tool as someone makes me. Whether I'm with my clients or with my honeybees, it's not about me. It's always about them. The key always lies in there hands. I'm just there to tell them where to turn it.

I wrote this book because, as part of my journey and story, my honeybees continue to be very influential in my life. They provide wonderful metaphors both for being a CEO and for being a coach. Not to mention I can bee very funny. (Okay I'll stop). It's my hope that these stories and observations will also be valuable for you on your journey. As you continue to learn and grow your business, you can refer to this book for inspiration and wisdom and maybe a reminder to stay present. Here's a recap of all the things we've covered:

**To Bee or Not to Bee.** I got into beekeeping as a hobby without realizing the impact it would have on my life. Never underestimate the value of being a well-rounded individual. Never underestimate the potential of having interests outside of your business. It helps you in numerous ways. For starters, it helps you to converse with people without an alternative motive of selling them something. When you have a wide range of topics on which you can talk confidently, your socials skills are more likely to expand and you will be able to gain the trust of other people. Not to mention, you have a good time while meeting them.

**A Photographer Who Can't Focus Is One Thing. A Beekeeper Who Can't Focus? Yikes!** Finding your focus is essential to the success of your business. Learning how to balance your focus among the big ideas, the practical realities, the timing, and growing your company will make all the difference in what you can achieve. It's as simple as keeping your eyes on the road. Yes, it helps to know where you're going and how you'll get there, but keeping your eyes on the path ahead of you keeps you on track and prevents you from derailing into a tragic loss.

**Bees Do Their Jobs . . . So Why Don't People Do Theirs?** Your business is made up of people, and so hiring the right people for the right jobs will make or break it. Putting your team members in the most appropriate roles, adopting the most effective communications practices, and helping your worker bees stay focused on their tasks will ensure your business runs smoothly. However, we all know its seldom as easy as that.

If you could simply press a button, move a few people around and have everything fixed, the entire premise of human resources and management would be rendered mute. What one must learn to do is to observe and understand their employees.

Evaluate their strengths and weaknesses and assign them tasks or positions accordingly.

**Why One Beehive Can't Have Two Queen Bees.** It can be lonely at the top, and it might be tempting to share the burden with another like-minded CEO. However, in the end, there really can be only one company culture and only one queen bee. By being (or "bee-ing") the only one in charge, you'll avoid the swarm, the mutiny, and the confusion.

There is a reason there is only one person chosen to be the president of a country. Theoretically it makes sense for many people to take charge and make decisions based on a collective opinion. However, when challenging matters come into play, one decisive and absolute opinion must exist that everyone abides by. This helps a decision to be made or else complete and utter chaos ensues.

**Why Do Some Hives Die and Some Hives Thrive?** There will always be certain factors that are beyond our control, but the story you choose to tell will affect the outcome of your business. Keeping an open mind is just as important as understanding who you are, knowing what your business is, and remaining true to your vision. Be secure in who you are, but also be ready to adapt to changing times.

Like a beehive, businesses are living organisms, evolving with the times and responding to the changing environment. This and my other books will provide you with a jumping-off point to begin your studies and better focus on your business. I encourage you to think about expanding your training, attending workshops, listening to podcasts, or giving yourself the gift of private business coaching.

This book has been my "why," but ultimately, it's about you. Why did you decide to start your business? What are your dreams for it, and what are you going to do to make those dreams a reality? How are you going to invest in the future you want for your business and your life? How hard will you work to "bee focused," stay present in the moment, and give yourself the greatest chance at success?

Every honey holds a different flavor, and every hive tells a story of survival. The story of your business has just begun. How will you survive, and how will you thrive? What comes next is totally up to you.

# Thank You

My purpose in writing this book is to help others in business and life. Your future is unlimited, focusing on what is important to you, always keeping that vision you always wanted.

As a gift from me, download one of my latest books for free on my website at *www.StrategistAdvisor.com.*

I will continue innovating and delivering extraordinary material with my world-class eLearning system and training videos. You can learn more about all of this on my business website *www.ScottProposki.com.*

Would you mind subscribing to my weekly podcast call the *3 O'clock Coffee Podcast*? We share extraordinary stories from successful people in business and life to inspire you. Listen for that one thing that will inspire you to do more in life and business. *www.3OclockCoffeePodcast.com*

Thank you,

*Scott Proposki*

# OTHER BOOKS BY
# SCOTT PROPOSKI

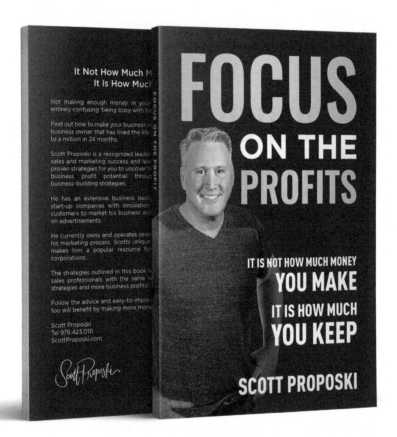

# Available on

# amazon.com

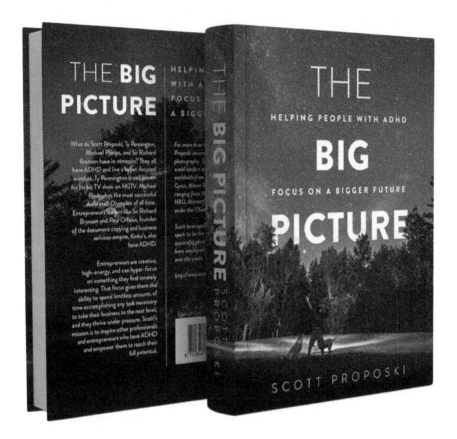

# www.ScottProposki.com

# Available as a Free Download
## at www.ScottProposki.com

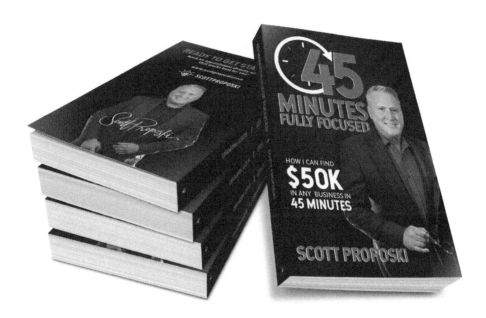

Made in the USA
Middletown, DE
18 August 2021